THE TEMPEST

WILLIAM SHAKESPEARE

NOTES BY MIKE GOULD

 Longman   York Press

YORK PRESS
322 Old Brompton Road, London SW5 9JH

PEARSON EDUCATION LIMITED
Edinburgh Gate, Harlow,
Essex CM20 2JE, United Kingdom
Associated companies, branches and representatives throughout the world

First published 2007

10 9 8 7 6 5 4 3 2 1

ISBN: 978–1–4058–5647–8

Illustrated by Chris Price; and Neil Gower (p. 6 c
Phototypeset by utimestwo, Northamptonshire
Printed in Great Britain by Henry Ling Limited, a

The author of these Notes is Mike Gould, an exp
He is also a former Head of English

CONTENTS

PREFACE

These York Notes aim to help you get the very best result in your Key Stage 3 test on *The Tempest*, but also enable you to enjoy your study, too. They will help you approach the test with confidence knowing that you have been given guidance on the **four key areas** you will be tested on:

- the characters and their motivation

- important ideas, themes and issues that run through the play

- the use of language in the text and its effects

- your understanding of the text in performance

THE TEST ITSELF

In the test you will be expected to answer a question on **two extracts** from *The Tempest*. The question will ask you about **one** of the four key areas above, for example:

Act I Scene 2 lines 322–75

Act V Scene 1 lines 256–99

What impression do we get of Caliban in these extracts?

You will have **45 minutes** to write on the extracts from *The Tempest*.

HOW THESE YORK NOTES WILL HELP

These Notes are divided up into sections which will help you answer questions such as the one above. You will find some background on Shakespeare – what do we know about him? What was it like going to the theatre in his day? Then, clear summaries of **every scene** will guide you through the play. In Part Three you'll find individual sections on the four key areas. Finally, these Notes will also help you with the test itself. You will be given guidance on exam technique, how to structure your answer, how to improve your level, and so on.

In the end, these Notes are designed to help you enjoy the play as you study it. They are not a substitute for reading the play but should help you make sense of Shakespeare's ideas and language, and gain a clear picture of how the characters behave, and why they act as they do.

The text used in these Notes is the Longman School Shakespeare edition, 2004.

PART ONE

INTRODUCTION

HOW TO STUDY A SHAKESPEARE PLAY

It may seem obvious, but it is important to remember that you are studying a play, a **text** that is meant to be performed. You should keep in mind that the words you see on the page are brought to life when they are acted out.

It is also important you keep in mind the four key areas you will be tested on. But what exactly do they mean?

❶ **CHARACTER** and **MOTIVATION**: this means what a **character** is *like* (ambitious? innocent? evil?), what they *do* (kill someone? fall in love? wear a disguise?) and *why* they behave in this way (is their motive to get revenge because they have been betrayed? or perhaps because they feel jealous?).

❷ **IDEAS, THEMES** and **ISSUES** in the play: this means the things that interested Shakespeare and he wanted the **audience** to think about. For example, what happens if someone desires something they can't have? Or, what problems do people have ruling a kingdom? It could also be the wider ideas that are explored in a play: different types of ambition, love, family conflict, death, and so on.

❸ The way Shakespeare uses **LANGUAGE** in the text and its effect: this means the different ways ideas in the play are expressed. For example, the use of powerful words or **phrases** to show how people feel, e.g. Caliban: 'A plague upon the tyrant that I serve!'; or the use of unusual **images**, e.g. Prospero to Ariel: 'Thou shalt be as free as mountain winds.'

❹ How the text works in **PERFORMANCE**: this means thinking about different ways the play might be staged and performed. For example, how would Ariel move around? How could the storm be presented on stage? How can Miranda's character be shown in the way she speaks, moves, or even how she dresses?

EXAMINER'S SECRET

Seeing *The Tempest* in **performance** will help you to understand and enjoy the play. If you can, try to go to a live performance on the stage, but if not there are several film or television versions available, such as the film directed by Derek Jarman in 1979.

EXAMINER'S SECRET

The Tempest is unusual amongst Shakespeare's plays in that it has more detailed **stage directions**, such as the descriptions of magic visions in Act III Scene 3. Think about how you can make use of these when looking at the text in performance.

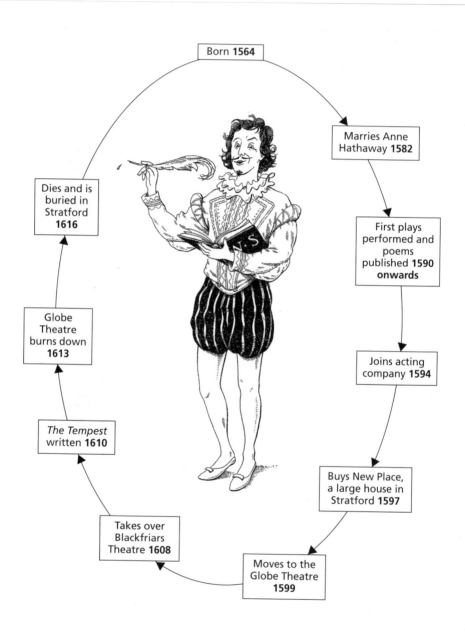

Born **1564**

Marries Anne Hathaway **1582**

First plays performed and poems published **1590 onwards**

Joins acting company **1594**

Buys New Place, a large house in Stratford **1597**

Moves to the Globe Theatre **1599**

Takes over Blackfriars Theatre **1608**

The Tempest written **1610**

Globe Theatre burns down **1613**

Dies and is buried in Stratford **1616**

WHO WAS SHAKESPEARE?

We actually know very little for certain about Shakespeare as no
personal records survive, such as diaries, letters and so on. What we
do have are references to him from other people, one of the earliest
being an insult: Shakespeare was called an 'upstart crow' – which
suggests the writer may have been rather jealous of his success! We
do know that Shakespeare came from quite a wealthy background
– his father was a successful merchant – and we also know that he
married young: at eighteen, to an older woman, Anne, who was
twenty-six. We know, too, that his son Hamnet died at the relatively
young age of eleven, and while it was common for children to die at
a young age during this period, we can imagine the sorrow this
event must have caused. Many of Shakespeare's plays explore
relationships between fathers and sons, and of course the name of
the hero in his most famous play, *Hamlet*, is remarkably close in
spelling to that of his own son.

It is likely, too, that Shakespeare spent many years away from Anne
in London, and while we don't know enough about their
relationship to say accurately whether the marriage was a happy one
or not, we can imagine that London would have seemed an
attractive place to him. It was a time of a great outburst in writing,
art and music (often referred to as the Renaissance) and Shakespeare
would probably have been excited by the range of new ideas and
possibilities available to playwrights at this time.

Most importantly, though, we need to understand that Shakespeare
was a working writer and actor, a skilled craftsman who was also
a clever businessman. He earned a living from his plays, which
were popular both with the rulers of the day (Elizabeth I and then
James I) and the ordinary public. His progress from budding writer
and actor to owner and manager of theatres, and the fact that he was
eventually able to buy the second largest house in his hometown of
Stratford, demonstrates how successful he was.

Finally, it is worth noting that Shakespeare was not just an actor and
playwright. He also wrote **poetry** and his Sonnets are almost as

 **DID YOU
KNOW?**

Renaissance is a
word that comes
from French and
means 'rebirth'. It is
used to describe a
very creative time
from the mid
fifteenth century to
the mid sixteenth
century, when
writers, artists and
musicians appeared
with new and
exciting ideas.

famous as his plays. What is most intriguing about them is that they seem to be addressed to two particular people. Many are addressed to a 'dark lady', while others are written to a young man, possibly a nobleman or lord. Like so many other things in Shakespeare's life, we do not know definitely *who* these people were, but the poems do give us a sense of Shakespeare being a very real person, writing about real relationships (falling in love, being rejected, getting angry, and so on), and not just someone from the past whom you are made to study by your teachers!

 DID YOU KNOW?

The original Globe Theatre in London was probably built in 1599, but was not strictly 'new' as it mostly consisted of timber from an old theatre in Blackfriars. This had to be carried across London to the south bank of the Thames!

GOING TO THE THEATRE IN SHAKESPEARE'S DAY

In Shakespeare's day, the theatre sometimes came to you! There were groups of travelling players who moved from town to town, and it is easy to forget that until the early to mid 1500s the idea of a theatre as a permanent public building was still relatively new. So you can imagine how exciting a trip to one of these new theatres was!

Once at the theatre, you could choose to pay for cheap tickets standing at the front as a 'groundling'. If you had more money you could pay for seats in the surrounding galleries. Wherever you were, sitting or standing, watching a Shakespeare play at the Globe, for example, would have been quite an experience! You might well have seen live animals, and heard **sound effects** such as thunder and a whole variety of music from drums and trumpets to whole orchestras! Plays such as *The Tempest* often contained dances, jokes and clowning, and the whole event would have been loud and vivid. As plays and theatres became more advanced, greater and greater use was made of trapdoors, and other ways of creating **special effects**, but the **scenery** itself remained quite basic for some years. **Costumes**, on the other hand, were generally magnificent. It may seem strange that there are sudden dances, songs, or magical appearances in some of Shakespeare's plays (sometimes with little connection to the **plot**!) but it is likely **audiences** would not have minded as they had come to the theatre for much more than just a good story. In any case, they must have enjoyed themselves for as many as 3,000 people often stood or sat for several hours to watch a **performance**, regardless of the weather!

In **contrast**, going to the theatre today is a more formal experience, although open-air theatres, such as the rebuilt Globe and the Regent's Park theatre, do still exist. We have also kept the idea of different prices of tickets, although it is very rare to stand to watch a performance nowadays. Scenery and **staging** are now very sophisticated in comparison.

The key point from all this is that Shakespeare's plays were written to be performed. His plays were designed as whole entertainment packages with opportunities to laugh, cry or gasp in shock or surprise. Keeping this in mind as you study or reflect on the play is quite useful, whether you are looking at **characters**, **themes**, **language** or **performance**.

 DID YOU KNOW?
There are several references to the 'globe' in Shakespeare's plays. Can you find a reference to it in Prospero's **monologue** starting on line 146 in Act IV Scene 1? What is he referring to here?

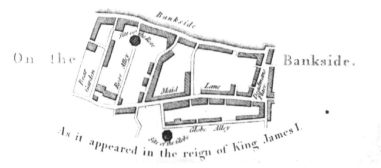

THE GLOBE THEATRE,

On the Bankside.

As it appeared in the reign of King James I.

PROSPERO'S CELL

Prospero, former Duke of Milan

Miranda, Prospero's daughter

Ferdinand, Alonso's son

Ariel, a spirit

ALONSO AND COMPANY

Alonso, King of Naples

Sebastian, Alonso's brother

Antonio, Prospero's brother

Gonzalo, an old councillor

Adrian and **Francisco**, lords

THE PLOTTERS

Caliban, a creature of the island

Stephano, Alonso's butler

Trinculo, Alonso's jester

THE SHIP'S COMPANY

Master

Boatswain

and other sailors

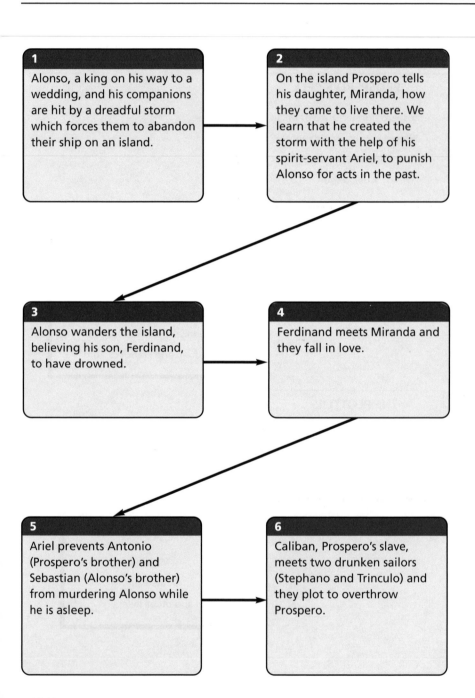

1
Alonso, a king on his way to a wedding, and his companions are hit by a dreadful storm which forces them to abandon their ship on an island.

2
On the island Prospero tells his daughter, Miranda, how they came to live there. We learn that he created the storm with the help of his spirit-servant Ariel, to punish Alonso for acts in the past.

3
Alonso wanders the island, believing his son, Ferdinand, to have drowned.

4
Ferdinand meets Miranda and they fall in love.

5
Ariel prevents Antonio (Prospero's brother) and Sebastian (Alonso's brother) from murdering Alonso while he is asleep.

6
Caliban, Prospero's slave, meets two drunken sailors (Stephano and Trinculo) and they plot to overthrow Prospero.

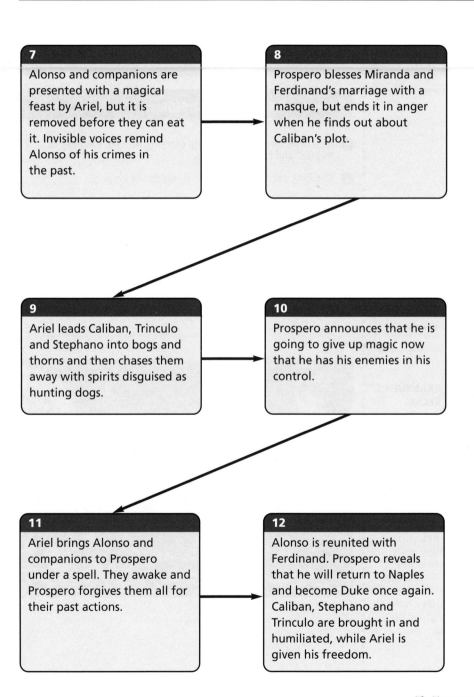

7

Alonso and companions are presented with a magical feast by Ariel, but it is removed before they can eat it. Invisible voices remind Alonso of his crimes in the past.

8

Prospero blesses Miranda and Ferdinand's marriage with a masque, but ends it in anger when he finds out about Caliban's plot.

9

Ariel leads Caliban, Trinculo and Stephano into bogs and thorns and then chases them away with spirits disguised as hunting dogs.

10

Prospero announces that he is going to give up magic now that he has his enemies in his control.

11

Ariel brings Alonso and companions to Prospero under a spell. They awake and Prospero forgives them all for their past actions.

12

Alonso is reunited with Ferdinand. Prospero reveals that he will return to Naples and become Duke once again. Caliban, Stephano and Trinculo are brought in and humiliated, while Ariel is given his freedom.

SUMMARIES

SCENE 1 – A SHIP IS HIT BY A STORM

❶ A terrible storm strikes a ship carrying Alonso, the King of Naples, and his companions.

❷ The king and the other lords abandon the ship.

The **scene** opens with the tempest of the title already in progress, as the Master and Boatswain shout out orders such as 'Take in the topsail!' (line 6). Gonzalo, a nobleman, finds comfort in the cheerful attitude of the Boatswain and can find 'no drowning mark upon him' (line 27). We find out that a king is on the ship, praying with his son below the deck, and that there are other noblemen on board. The scene ends with general confusion and the suggestion that the boat is about to break up and sink.

CHECKPOINT 1

Why would this have been a difficult scene to stage in Shakespeare's day?

EXAMINER'S SECRET

Often, small details can help convey the *effect* of a scene. If you can pick up on these, then this shows close reading of the **text**. For example, note how many exclamation marks and **imperative** verbs there are in this scene. These create the feeling of short, sharp cries which fits the action on the ship.

Action and chaos

This opening scene is one of action. When thinking about the **staging** and **performance**, look at how Shakespeare creates a mood of confusion. The scene opens with the *'tempestuous noise of thunder and lightning'*, various **characters** enter and **exit**, and there are shouts and cries from characters on stage mixed with voices *'off-stage'*. Even the simple **stage direction** *'Enter Mariners, wet'* (after line 47) adds to the general picture. Yet despite the hurried comings-and-goings we do find out the important information that the ship carries a king and his son. We are even given early clues about certain characters. Gonzalo is hopeful of survival – and this optimism will be repeated later in the play. Antonio and Sebastian, on the other hand, shout insults at the Boatswain, calling him an 'incharitable dog' (line 39) and 'insolent noisemaker' (line 41). This perhaps prepares us for the unpleasantness these men will show in future scenes.

SCENE 2 (LINES 1–186) – PROSPERO TELLS MIRANDA HER LIFE HISTORY

❶ On the island, Miranda questions her father about the storm and the ship.

❷ Prospero reassures her and then tells her about how they both came to be there.

This long scene opens with Prospero assuring Miranda that no one has been hurt in the storm that he has raised. He then tells her the facts about how they came to be on the island. Prospero informs her that twelve years earlier he had been the Duke of Milan, but, being more interested in study and books, he had allowed his brother, Antonio, to plot against him with the King of Naples, Alonso. A 'treacherous army' was 'levied' (line 128) and Prospero was thrown out of government. He and Miranda were put in a small boat and cast out to sea. They only survived due to the kindness of a nobleman called Gonzalo who provided them with 'rich garments, linens, stuffs, and necessaries' (line 164). We learn that Prospero

GLOSSARY

no drowning mark i.e. he is not likely to drown

tempestuous stormy

incharitable unkind

insolent rude

levied gathered

stuffs household items

DID YOU KNOW?

The storm Prospero describes might have been based on a real shipwreck of a boat called the *Sea Venture* off the coast of America in 1609. People became fascinated by one survivor's account of Bermuda, the exotic island he ended up on.

DID YOU KNOW?

The idea of an older man, Prospero, looking back at past events is interesting because *The Tempest* was almost certainly the last play Shakespeare wrote on his own, around 1610. The plays he wrote after that were probably written jointly with other writers. Perhaps, like Prospero, he had had enough of controlling everything himself!

created the storm when the chance came to get revenge on those who had been responsible for his exile from Milan. At the end of his speech, Prospero appears to cast a spell on Miranda, sending her to sleep.

A tale to cure deafness?

The opening to this **scene** is in complete **contrast** to Act I Scene 1. Whilst that was all commands, insults and action, this seems generally thoughtful and calm. The purpose of this part of Scene 2 is to explain the background to the storm for the **audience**, but Shakespeare himself seems aware that there is a lot of information to be provided. Although Miranda is clearly moved by what she hears, her father's account is very long. It is possible Shakespeare wanted to break up Prospero's speech in order to keep the audience interested. Therefore, when Prospero asks his daughter, 'Dost thou hear?' (line 106), he is perhaps making sure the audience is paying attention as well as Miranda! But remember, we do find out important information in this scene, and we are given Prospero's **motivation**: revenge. Shakespeare alerts us to the importance of what Prospero says with Miranda's comment 'Your tale, sir, would cure deafness' (line 107). This suggests that the story is so fascinating it would break through deaf ears!

SCENE 2 (LINES 187–305) – PROSPERO'S HELPER

❶ Ariel gives an account of the storm and what has happened.

❷ Prospero orders Ariel to carry out further tasks for him.

Ariel (the spirit who serves Prospero) describes how he created the storm, and its effect on the ship's crew, the king and his companions. He tells Prospero that no one has been hurt, but that he has 'dispersed them about the isle' (line 220) and that Ferdinand (the prince) has been separated from his father, Alonso. The ship has been placed 'safely in the harbour' in a 'deep nook' (lines 226–7) and the crew are asleep under a spell. Ariel then asks Prospero to grant him the freedom he says he has been promised, but Prospero refuses. He tells Ariel that his work is not yet finished. He also reminds him that it was he, Prospero, who first freed Ariel from imprisonment from 'the foul witch Sycorax' (line 258), the mother of Prospero's other slave, Caliban. Prospero warns him that if he complains again he will 'rend an oak and peg thee in his knotty entrails' (lines 294–5). In other words, he will imprison him again inside a tree. If he behaves himself, Prospero will release him in two days' time. Ariel promises to do as he is told in future without making a fuss.

CHECKPOINT 2

What reason is given in the play why Ariel might have ended up imprisoned in the tree forever if Prospero hadn't come to the rescue?

Master and servant

We meet Ariel for the first time, and soon realise what magic powers he (or should that be 'it'?) has. Ariel can fly, become invisible, and change shape – even separate himself ('divide' as he calls it). No wonder he is so useful to Prospero. What is most interesting is their relationship. They both need each other: Ariel needs Prospero because he has the power to free him (or keep him as a servant/slave); and Prospero needs Ariel to carry out his plans.

CHECKPOINT 3

What sort of spirit is Ariel? Do we ever find out if he is mortal, or has human feelings at any stage in the play?

Scene 2 (lines 306–75) – Prospero and Caliban

1 Prospero orders Caliban to appear.

2 Caliban argues violently with Prospero over who owns the island.

Prospero wakes Miranda and they meet Caliban who angrily shouts insults at them. Prospero warns him that he will be punished with painful 'cramps' and 'side-stitches' (lines 326–7) in the night as a result. Caliban argues that the island originally belonged to him, and that Prospero was once kind to him. Prospero's response is that he cared for him until Caliban tried to rape Miranda. She herself reminds Caliban that she had once felt pity for him and had taught him to speak, but that he had repaid her with 'vile' behaviour

GLOSSARY

dispersed separated and placed in different locations

nook inlet

rend split

entrails insides (normally of a stomach)

CHECKPOINT 4

How are we supposed to feel about Caliban?

(line 359). Prospero orders Caliban to fetch fuel for them, and reminds him to do it without complaint or he will be punished. Caliban leaves, fearing Prospero's power.

You taught me language

Several of the key **themes** in the play can be found in this short exchange. Firstly, there is the idea of *nature* and *nurture.* In other words, if someone is born evil (they are evil by nature), can they be made good by being nurtured (by being cared for and encouraged)? Caliban is taught how to speak but he tells Miranda, 'You taught me language and my profit on't is I know how to curse' (lines 365–6). In other words, he was educated but he used that education for unpleasant behaviour. This theme is closely linked to *power* and *government.* Caliban claims the island is his, as he was on it first – but that he is now a slave.

 **EXAMINER'S SECRET**

It's easy to ignore Shakespeare's songs and think that they are unimportant. However, apart from telling us about **characters** they can reflect **themes** and ideas, and display wonderful language. 'Full fathom five …' uses **alliteration** which creates a spell-like **tone** that fits with the magic of the play.

SCENE 2 (LINES 376–505) – MIRANDA AND FERDINAND MEET

❶ **Ariel leads Ferdinand into Prospero's 'cell'.**

❷ **Prospero arranges for Miranda to meet Ferdinand.**

❸ **They begin to fall in love.**

Ariel leads Ferdinand on to the stage with magical music, and then sings a new song, 'Full fathom five …' (lines 399 onwards). Ferdinand realises it is about his father. Prospero shows Ferdinand to Miranda and she is enchanted by what she sees. They then meet face-to-face and begin to fall in love, although Ferdinand is sad because he believes that his father and the rest of his companions are dead. Prospero decides that Ferdinand must earn Miranda's love, and pretends that Ferdinand is a 'traitor' (line 464) who will be imprisoned and enslaved. Ferdinand draws his sword to challenge Prospero, but Prospero puts a spell on him so he cannot move. Miranda begs her father to show him mercy, and assures Ferdinand that her father is not as unkind as he appears.

GLOSSARY

fathom a measure of the depth of water

TEST YOURSELF (ACT I)

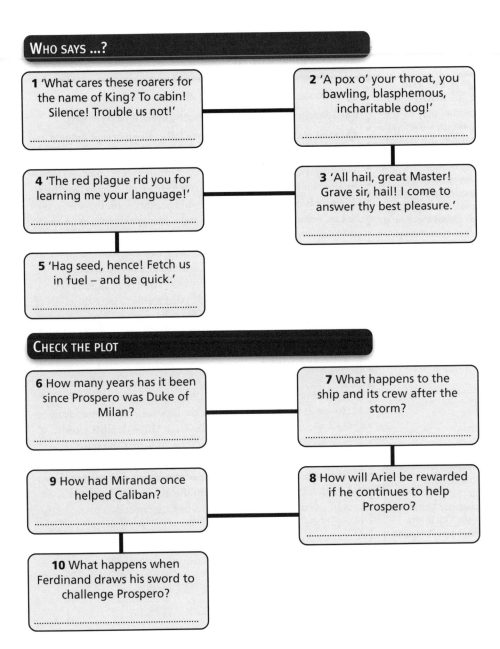

WHO SAYS ...?

1 'What cares these roarers for the name of King? To cabin! Silence! Trouble us not!'

....

2 'A pox o' your throat, you bawling, blasphemous, incharitable dog!'

....

4 'The red plague rid you for learning me your language!'

....

3 'All hail, great Master! Grave sir, hail! I come to answer thy best pleasure.'

....

5 'Hag seed, hence! Fetch us in fuel – and be quick.'

....

CHECK THE PLOT

6 How many years has it been since Prospero was Duke of Milan?

....

7 What happens to the ship and its crew after the storm?

....

9 How had Miranda once helped Caliban?

....

8 How will Ariel be rewarded if he continues to help Prospero?

....

10 What happens when Ferdinand draws his sword to challenge Prospero?

....

Check your answers on p. 77.

SCENE 1 (LINES 1–191) – ALONSO AND COMPANIONS DISCUSS THEIR SITUATION

DID YOU KNOW?

Another play by Shakespeare which features the idea of a young hero who may or may not have drowned is *Twelfth Night*. It opens with a young girl called Viola on a beach in a strange land. She has survived a shipwreck, but is comforted by being told that her twin brother, who she fears is drowned, had been seen swimming strongly.

1 Gonzalo attempts to comfort Alonso.

2 Gonzalo describes how he would govern if he were king.

3 Ariel plays music and everyone falls asleep except Antonio and Sebastian.

The king, his brother (Sebastian) and Prospero's brother (Antonio) are now on the island. Gonzalo tries to reassure Alonso that their situation is not as bad as it seems, and another lord, Francisco, says he saw Ferdinand swimming strongly after the shipwreck. Alonso is not convinced, and remains in a state of dark despair. Despite insults and jokes at his expense by Sebastian and Antonio, Gonzalo reflects on what he would do if he were ruler of the island, or 'commonwealth' as he calls it (line 143). Ariel then appears and plays '*solemn music*' (after line 176) that seems to have the effect of putting everyone to sleep, except for Sebastian and Antonio.

Gonzalo's island

Gonzalo's ideas about how he would rule the island link in with the **theme** of power and government we have seen elsewhere. However, the place he talks about does not seem very realistic. He says, 'all men' would be 'idle' (line 150) – in other words, have no jobs – and women would be 'innocent and pure' (line 151), and there would be no king! He would allow nature to develop on its own without use of machinery. This picture is perhaps rather like an unreal, **mythical** paradise – perhaps even a Garden of Eden – and fits in with Gonzalo's own optimistic **character**.

CHECKPOINT 5

How close is Gonzalo's view to what the island is really like in the play? Has Prospero treated the island in this way?

SCENE 1 (LINES 192–321) – THE PLOT TO KILL ALONSO

1 Sebastian and Antonio plot to murder Alonso and Gonzalo.

2 Ariel enters and warns Gonzalo.

3 Gonzalo and Alonso wake up before Sebastian and Antonio can act.

4 Ariel leaves to report what he has seen to Prospero.

Once Alonso, Gonzalo and the other lords are asleep, Antonio suggests to Sebastian that Sebastian could kill the king his brother and take his place. This mirrors what Antonio tried to do to Prospero, his brother. The plan suits them both as it will free Antonio from paying 'tribute' (a tax) to Alonso (line 285). They are sure Ferdinand is dead, so he will not stand in their way either. They decide to kill Gonzalo, too, as he seems loyal to Alonso. However, just as they draw their swords, Ariel enters and sings a warning into Gonzalo's ear. He awakes and in turn warns Alonso. The king asks Sebastian and Antonio why their swords are drawn, and they invent an excuse – that they heard 'a herd of lions' (line 308). They decide to leave, and **exit** the stage with their weapons drawn. Ariel leaves, too, in order to let Prospero know about Sebastian and Antonio's treachery.

Sleepy language

When Antonio first suggests that Sebastian might take his brother's crown, Sebastian says, 'What, art thou waking?' (line 201) – in other words, 'Are you talking nonsense?' Antonio continues the idea of sleep by telling Sebastian that he is letting his 'fortune sleep' (line 208). By this he means that Sebastian's future riches and power are asleep but he could wake them up by killing his brother. Finally, Sebastian answers by saying that if Antonio is talking in his sleep, his 'snores' have 'meaning' (line 210) which shows he is beginning to understand what Antonio is planning! This **extended metaphor** (a comparison that is stretched over several lines) is typical of Shakespeare's way of exploring ideas.

CHECKPOINT 6

Why do you think Ariel prevents Antonio and Sebastian from killing Alonso and Gonzalo?

 DID YOU KNOW?

Sleep is very important in Shakespeare's plays. Sometimes it is used **symbolically** to represent ideas such as death (for example, in *Macbeth*). On other occasions it allows Shakespeare to show dreams or nightmares on stage, as in *Richard III* when Richard sees the ghosts of all his victims the night before a battle.

GLOSSARY

commonwealth a state governed by all the people, rather than a single ruler

SCENE 2 – CALIBAN JOINS FORCES WITH TRINCULO AND STEPHANO

CHECKPOINT 7

Why does Caliban know the island so well? Is there any other **character** who can find their way around it like him?

EXAMINER'S SECRET

Places can have 'character' too. You can show *insight* into the play by looking at the character of the island. Is it kind and inviting, or cruel and somewhere people want to escape from? Does everyone have the same attitude to it?

❶ Caliban is found by Trinculo who hides with him.

❷ Stephano appears and Trinculo reveals himself.

❸ Caliban offers to serve them and show them the island.

When Trinculo appears, Caliban hides, thinking he might be one of Prospero's spirits sent to 'torment' him (line 15). There is a sound of thunder and Trinculo decides to join Caliban under his 'gaberdine' cloak (line 38) until the worst of the storm has passed. A drunken Stephano then appears, and seeing Trinculo and Caliban's legs sticking out under the cloak thinks he is looking at a monster with four legs. When Caliban speaks, Stephano pours wine into his mouth, but Trinculo soon recognises Stephano's voice and reveals himself to his shipmate. Caliban now presents himself to both men and decides to serve Stephano, whom he calls a 'brave god' (line 114). Trinculo and Stephano exchange stories about how they survived the storm, while Caliban offers to show them 'every fertile inch' of the island (line 143). Caliban begins to plan his revenge on Prospero. The three leave, singing drunkenly.

Fun and games?

On the surface, this is simply a very funny scene with **slapstick humour** that Shakespearean **audiences** would have loved. Shakespeare suggests that Trinculo and Caliban are lying 'top to tail' to form the monster. This means that one of the monster's voices, the 'backward' one, comes from his backside, whilst the 'forward' one comes from his mouth (lines 89–90)! The **physical comedy** and **play on words** make this a great scene to perform.

Ownership of the island

Caliban's vivid language, describing the 'jay's nest', 'nimble marmoset' and 'clust'ring filberts' (lines 165–7) gives a lively picture of the island. However, this **scene** sets in motion the **subplot** – the conspiracy to kill Prospero and make Stephano king of the island. Caliban's hatred of Prospero is stressed in his furious words 'A plague upon the tyrant that I serve!' (line 157) and his account of the torment he has suffered. In this way, the **themes** of power and government, and justice and revenge are developed through what Caliban says and does.

CHECKPOINT 8

What other animals or creatures are mentioned in the play?

GLOSSARY

gaberdine a type of thick cloth used in coats

marmoset a small monkey with a hairy tail

filberts a type of hazelnut

Now take a break!

WHO SAYS ...?

1 'O ... what strange fish hath made his meal on thee?'

....

2 'I would with such perfection govern, sir, t'excel the Golden Age.'

....

4 'All the infections that the sun sucks up from bogs, fens, flats, on Prosper fall.'

....

3 'My strong imagination sees a crown dropping upon thy head.'

....

5 'Trinculo, the King and all our companions else being drowned, we will inherit here.'

....

CHECK THE PLOT

6 Why does Francisco think Ferdinand might still be alive?

....

7 How would Antonio benefit from Alonso's death?

....

9 How does Trinculo know it is Stephano?

....

8 Why does Trinculo decide to seek shelter under Caliban's cloak?

....

10 Why does Caliban decide to serve Stephano?

....

Check your answers on p. 77.

SCENE 1 – FERDINAND AND MIRANDA DECLARE THEIR LOVE

❶ **Ferdinand carries out work for Prospero.**

❷ **Miranda appears and they express their love for each other.**

❸ **Prospero, having watched them, leaves to carry out his other plans.**

This short **scene** opens with Ferdinand carrying wood for Prospero. This leads him to compare Prospero's harshness to Miranda's kindness. Miranda enters and tries to make him work less hard, unaware that Prospero is watching them both from a distance, unseen.

Prospero realises that Miranda has fallen in love and is 'infected' (line 31). Ferdinand asks Miranda her name, and then reveals that the moment he saw her, he fell for her. They agree to be bound together in marriage, and take each other's hand, before leaving in different directions. Prospero admits, rather strangely, that he is not as 'glad' (line 92) as they are, but his 'rejoicing' (line 94) could not be any greater! He departs to continue his plans for his enemies.

> **CHECKPOINT 9**
>
> Prospero uses the word 'infected' to describe how Miranda feels about Ferdinand. What does this tell us about Prospero's view of her love for Ferdinand?

DID YOU KNOW?

In a film made in 1979 Miranda was played by a young punk-like pop-star called Toyah Wilcox, with dyed, multi-coloured hair. How might this have made the audience view Miranda?

Miranda's innocence

What are the **audience** to make of Miranda here? She admits she has never seen another woman's face, except in her own 'glass' (line 50) and no other man than her father, yet she willingly falls for Ferdinand. Unlike Ferdinand, who admits to having met 'full many a lady' (line 39), she is entirely innocent. Is perhaps the point of the scene to **contrast** her decency, kindness and trust with the various other **characters** and relationships elsewhere in the play?

SCENE 2 – CALIBAN'S CONSPIRACY

EXAMINER'S SECRET

Be careful with what you say about Ariel. Because he is not human, do not make the mistake of summing him up as one thing only. Remember, he can change from **scene** to scene, so look carefully at how he behaves and speaks in the set scenes (if he is in them).

❶ Caliban, Stephano and Trinculo drink and argue.

❷ Ariel imitates Trinculo's voice, causing Stephano to strike Trinculo.

❸ Caliban describes how they can murder Prospero.

❹ Ariel plays a tune on a pipe and the three conspirators follow it off-stage.

The three new companions enter, drinking heavily. Ariel, invisible, imitates Trinculo's voice. This makes it appear that he is arguing with Stephano and Caliban. Stephano orders the innocent Trinculo not to interrupt, or abuse Caliban, but when Ariel imitates him again, Stephano strikes poor Trinculo. Caliban explains how they can destroy Prospero by seizing his books and can 'batter his skull', 'paunch him with a stake' or 'cut his wezand' (lines 88–9) using a knife. Eventually, having agreed their plan, they start to sing, but are interrupted by Ariel playing a tune on a pipe. Amazed, they stop, and Caliban tells them the island has many strange, but beautiful, sounds. Eventually, they follow the music which leads them **off-stage**.

The Island

Caliban's speech about the island is particularly interesting because it gives one of the most beautiful speeches of the play to a 'monster' and would-be murderer. For a moment, we see another Caliban. He is almost child-like and innocent, a dreamer who hears 'sounds and sweet airs' (line 133) and a 'thousand twangling instruments' (line 134). It is difficult to feel anything but pity and sympathy for him at this point.

EXAMINER'S SECRET

It is easy to think of one character being 'good', another 'evil'. But make sure you base what you say on *evidence*. Can we really think of Caliban as a villain when he makes such a beautiful speech about the island?

SCENE 3 – A GHOSTLY FEAST AND A GUILTY PAST

1. **Alonso and companions rest.**
2. **Magical spirits produce a banquet, but it vanishes when the men try to eat.**
3. **Ariel appears and powerfully reminds Alonso and the others of their guilt.**
4. **Unnerved, they leave.**

Alonso has given up hope that his son is still alive, having searched the island. Seeing how tired Gonzalo and the king are, Sebastian and Antonio decide to attempt to kill them during the night. Spirits then appear with a wonderful banquet, with an unseen Prospero watching. As Alonso stands up to start eating, thunder and lightning strike and Ariel appears as a terrifying winged '*Harpy*' (after line 52). The food is removed and he speaks to Alonso, Sebastian and Antonio, saying they are 'three men of sin' (line 53). When they draw their swords, Ariel makes them too heavy to lift. He then vanishes, and spirits remove the table. Alonso believes he has heard the name of Prospero, and begins to feel guilt for his past deeds. Everyone leaves, their minds confused by what they have experienced.

DID YOU KNOW?

In Greek **myth**, a harpy was originally a winged hawk-like spirit, associated with death and snatching food.

GLOSSARY
glass mirror
paunch stab in the stomach
wezand throat

CHECKPOINT 10

Do you think that
Shakespeare
intends Ariel to be
male or female, or
neither? Does it
matter?

Powerful staging

This can be a hugely dramatic **scene** which **audiences** in
Shakespeare's day would have loved, with spirits and magical
appearances. However, apart from the dramatic events, the scene
is important because Ariel becomes a very different type of
figure. Before this, he has been rather imp-like and playful, but
he now becomes a terrifying creature, representing justice and
revenge. This can be quite a challenge for an actor or actress
playing the part of Ariel, as he or she will have to go from
imitating Trinculo's voice for comic effect in Act III Scene 2 to
becoming a frightening harpy in this scene.

Now take a break!

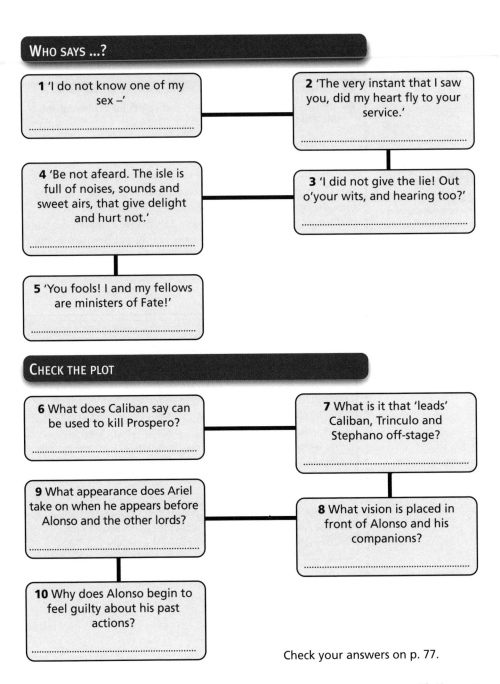

WHO SAYS ...?

1 'I do not know one of my sex –'
....

2 'The very instant that I saw you, did my heart fly to your service.'
....

4 'Be not afeard. The isle is full of noises, sounds and sweet airs, that give delight and hurt not.'
....

3 'I did not give the lie! Out o'your wits, and hearing too?'
....

5 'You fools! I and my fellows are ministers of Fate!'
....

CHECK THE PLOT

6 What does Caliban say can be used to kill Prospero?
....

7 What is it that 'leads' Caliban, Trinculo and Stephano off-stage?
....

9 What appearance does Ariel take on when he appears before Alonso and the other lords?
....

8 What vision is placed in front of Alonso and his companions?
....

10 Why does Alonso begin to feel guilty about his past actions?
....

Check your answers on p. 77.

Scene 1 (lines 1–163) – A marriage gift

1. **Prospero grants Miranda's hand in marriage to Ferdinand.**
2. **He puts on a show – a 'masque' – of spirits for Ferdinand and Miranda.**

Prospero apologises to Ferdinand for his rough treatment and grants him Miranda's hand in marriage. He then presents a 'masque' or show, involving several spirits in the form of goddesses, such as Iris, Ceres and Juno, as celebration for the coming wedding. They bless the two young lovers and then further spirits arrive and perform a *'graceful dance'* (after line 138) before Prospero suddenly remembers Caliban's plot. The spirits vanish, and Prospero seems angry. He makes a speech about the show he has created and links it to his own life. Finally, he tells the two lovers to go inside until he has calmed down.

DID YOU KNOW?

Masques in Shakespeare's time were usually lavish, dramatic entertainments often spoken in **verse**, usually performed by masked actors in the role of well-known figures from **myths** or legends.

A different language

The goddesses who perform for Miranda and Ferdinand represent hope for the future, and the idea of rebirth. Iris is goddess of the rainbow, Ceres, goddess of the harvest, and Juno is queen of all the gods. Iris speaks of nature's goodness – of 'rich leas, of wheat, rye, barley' (lines 60–1) – while Ceres blesses the lovers, telling them 'Scarcity and want shall shun you; Ceres' blessing so is on you' (lines 116–17). However, it is worth noting that the **rhymed couplets**, often in shorter lines like the one above, are in clear contrast to most of the speech in the play. The use of **rhyme** separates this magical show from the 'real' speaking in the play. The words also sound rather like a song, a hymn or a spell which makes the show seem like a blessing, or perhaps some sort of formal service.

Our revels now are ended

Prospero's **monologue** (lines 146–63) is rather sad in **tone**. It has often been seen as Shakespeare talking about himself, near the end of his life. He refers to the unimportance of man's creations when he predicts that 'the cloud-capped towers, the gorgeous palaces, the solemn temples, the great globe itself … shall dissolve' (lines 152–4). It is as if Shakespeare, through Prospero, is telling the **audience**: 'I made these things, but in the end it's all just a show and nothing can last forever.' What's important in the *play* is that this speech shows a different side to Prospero – perhaps a tired, older man, ready to go home to Milan.

SCENE 1 (LINES 164–262) – DEALING WITH CALIBAN

1 **Ariel reports back to Prospero about Caliban and company.**

2 **The plotters arrive at Prospero's cell.**

3 **Prospero and Ariel order spirits disguised as hunting dogs to chase them away.**

Ariel tells Prospero what Caliban, Stephano and Trinculo have been doing and how he has 'charmed' them (line 178) so that they have been thrown into filthy water, and dragged through thorns and gorse. The **plotters** arrive, unaware they are being watched. They prepare to enter Prospero's home but the two men are distracted by beautiful garments on a line, placed there by Prospero and Ariel. Forgetting their plan, they try to steal the clothes but Prospero and Ariel chase them away, using spirits disguised in the form of hunting dogs.

DID YOU KNOW?

The 'great globe' is often seen to be a reference to the actual theatre, the Globe. Shakespeare often made references in his plays to the idea that life was rather like a play in the theatre. In *As You Like It* one of the characters says, 'All the world's a stage'. In *Macbeth*, Macbeth says that a man is a 'walking player who struts and frets his hour upon the stage'.

CHECKPOINT 11

Do you think there is any significance in the names of the hunting dogs called out by Prospero and Ariel?

GLOSSARY
leas farmland
shun ignore

Caliban, the sensible!

Caliban begins to realise in this **scene** that the man he has chosen to follow is not much more than a drunken fool. Stephano and Trinculo are more concerned about losing their wine – an 'infinite loss' as Stephano calls it (line 209) – and flashy clothes, than ruling the island. Caliban's attitude is summed up when he tells Trinculo, 'Let it alone, thou fool! It is but trash' (line 222).

CHECKPOINT 12

Do you think that Prospero is ever really in danger from the plotters?

GLOSSARY

infinite too large to measure

Now take a break!

TEST YOURSELF (ACT IV)

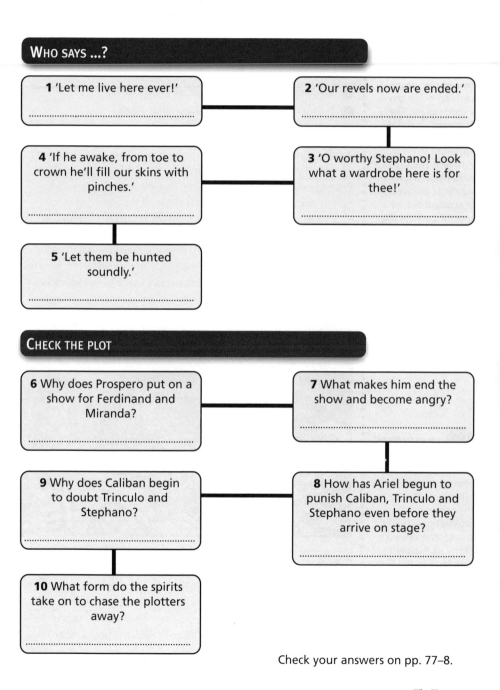

WHO SAYS ...?

1 'Let me live here ever!'

....

2 'Our revels now are ended.'

....

4 'If he awake, from toe to crown he'll fill our skins with pinches.'

....

3 'O worthy Stephano! Look what a wardrobe here is for thee!'

....

5 'Let them be hunted soundly.'

....

CHECK THE PLOT

6 Why does Prospero put on a show for Ferdinand and Miranda?

....

7 What makes him end the show and become angry?

....

9 Why does Caliban begin to doubt Trinculo and Stephano?

....

8 How has Ariel begun to punish Caliban, Trinculo and Stephano even before they arrive on stage?

....

10 What form do the spirits take on to chase the plotters away?

....

Check your answers on pp. 77–8.

EXAMINER'S SECRET

One of the ways you can break down a long speech like Prospero's is to take a copy of it and highlight in different colours either powerful words or **phrases** that stand out, or specific parts of the speech – for example, all nouns to do with Nature (like 'oak') and all verbs to do with movement (for example, 'chase').

SCENE 1 (LINES 1–100) – PROSPERO MAKES PREPARATIONS

1 Ariel reports back to Prospero on his enemies.

2 Prospero says he is going to abandon magic.

3 Alonso, Gonzalo and companions are brought to Prospero's cell.

Ariel gives a detailed report on the king and his companions, and says that Prospero might feel sorry for them if he could see them. Prospero says he will release them from the spell they are under. Left on his own, he gives a speech about all the spirits who have assisted him in creating the storm and other effects. He announces that he is going to abandon magic. Ariel reappears with Alonso and the others, who are under a spell. Prospero speaks to each one in turn accusing them of their crimes, and then forgives them. Slowly, they start to wake, while Prospero dresses in the robes which he wore when he was ruler of Milan.

EXAMINER'S SECRET

Think about a **character**'s *history* when you discuss his or her **motivations**. It was books that caused many of Prospero's problems in the first place, as it was his love of reading and learning that made him neglect his duties as a ruler. Perhaps he has now learned his lesson.

Giving up magic

Prospero's speech (lines 33–57) is a key moment in the play. He rejects magic, which has allowed him to dim the 'noontide sun' (line 41) and raise the 'mutinous winds' (line 41). He tells us he is going to 'drown' his book (line 57), which is presumably his book of spells and charms.

SCENE 1 (LINES 101–215) – FORGIVING ENEMIES

❶ **The king and his companions awake and face Prospero.**

❷ **Alonso asks Prospero for forgiveness.**

❸ **Prospero forgives Antonio and Sebastian.**

❹ **He invites the visitors to look inside his cell.**

Prospero welcomes Alonso and Gonzalo who are overcome with surprise. Prospero tells Antonio and Sebastian that if he wanted he could reveal their treachery towards Alonso, but he will not do so now. Instead he forgives them, but demands his dukedom back from Antonio. Alonso mourns the loss of his son, and Prospero says he has lost a daughter too. He then tells the king that as he has given him back his dukedom, he will give something back to Alonso in return. He asks Alonso to look inside his cell.

The same old Antonio?

Often, questions on Shakespeare's plays will relate to how a character changes or develops. But what about Antonio? At the start of the play, we know Antonio is a villain because we are told he stole Prospero's dukedom. Prospero says in this **scene** that to call him 'brother / Would even infect my mouth' (lines 130–1), suggesting even his name is poisonous. Yet, despite Prospero's harsh words, Antonio shows no guilt or regret for his treatment of Prospero or his plot to kill Alonso, which Prospero decides not to reveal for Antonio's sake. Is Shakespeare saying that however hard you try, some people will always be bad? This is connected to the **theme** of nature versus nurture (see 'You taught me language', p. 18).

CHECKPOINT 13

In what way are Alonso's words about his lost son, and Prospero's answer a good example of dramatic irony?

GLOSSARY

mutinous wild and rebellious

SCENE 1 (LINES 216–318) – READY TO DEPART

❶ Prospero reveals Miranda and Ferdinand playing chess.

❷ Ariel brings in the ship's crew, unharmed.

❸ Caliban, Stephano and Trinculo are brought in.

❹ Prospero gives Ariel one last task and then frees him.

Prospero shows Alonso that his son is alive and it becomes clear that he and Miranda have fallen in love. They will marry and become future rulers of Naples and Milan. The Boatswain and the rest of the sailors arrive, full of tales of how the broken ship has been miraculously mended. Finally, the three **plotters** are driven in by Ariel, the two men still wearing the clothes they stole. Caliban regrets having thought a foolish drunkard could become king, and says he will work hard for Prospero's pardon. Prospero asks Ariel to create winds that will guide the ships back to Italy, and says that once he has done that, he can be free.

EPILOGUE

❶ Prospero remains on stage.

❷ He asks the audience to 'release' him by applauding.

Prospero, or the actor playing Prospero, speaks alone to the **audience** and asks them to let him go back to Naples, or perhaps back to his dressing-room! He says his purpose was to entertain them, and asks for their 'indulgence' (line 20) in letting him go.

Leaving the island – or the theatre?

In this Epilogue, Prospero asks the audience to let him go by clapping. Of course, in the *play* Prospero does not need to be released by the audience, but the actor playing him is saying it is time for him to return to his dressing-room! The magic Shakespeare has created on the stage is about to end in the same way as the 'real' magic Prospero has created on the island.

CHECKPOINT 14

Is there any significance in the fact that Miranda and Ferdinand are playing chess? Think about the aim of the game, and the background to the play.

DID YOU KNOW?

Epilogue comes from the Greek 'epilogos' – meaning 'conclusion'. You might expect it is always spoken by the grandest, or most powerful character, but this is not always the case. In *A Midsummer Night's Dream* it is spoken by a spirit called 'Puck', who is a little like Ariel.

GLOSSARY

indulgence favour, permission

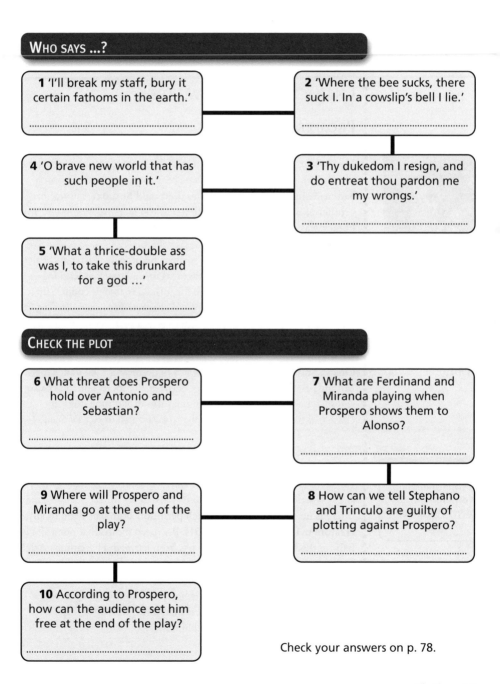

WHO SAYS ...?

1 'I'll break my staff, bury it certain fathoms in the earth.'

....

2 'Where the bee sucks, there suck I. In a cowslip's bell I lie.'

....

4 'O brave new world that has such people in it.'

....

3 'Thy dukedom I resign, and do entreat thou pardon me my wrongs.'

....

5 'What a thrice-double ass was I, to take this drunkard for a god ...'

....

CHECK THE PLOT

6 What threat does Prospero hold over Antonio and Sebastian?

....

7 What are Ferdinand and Miranda playing when Prospero shows them to Alonso?

....

9 Where will Prospero and Miranda go at the end of the play?

....

8 How can we tell Stephano and Trinculo are guilty of plotting against Prospero?

....

10 According to Prospero, how can the audience set him free at the end of the play?

....

Check your answers on p. 78.

PART THREE

COMMENTARY

CHARACTER AND MOTIVATION

PROSPERO

Twelve years before he arrived on the island Prospero was Duke of Milan. Then his brother Antonio, with the help of Alonso (the King of Naples), rebelled and took his place. Prospero's love of books had made him neglect his duties as duke, and he did not notice his brother plotting against him until it was too late. Prospero says, 'my library was dukedom large enough' (I.2.109–10).

Powerful
Magical
Stern

Once he arrived on the island, Prospero became its master and ruler, and his love of books and studying was turned towards learning about magic. By the time the play begins, he is able to conjure up storms and spirits, and cast spells and charms over others. In fact, one of the main ways we see Prospero is as a sorcerer or magician, with the power to raise a tempest which he does at the beginning of the play. Prospero's magical power is used on many other occasions. One example is the visions he creates of goddesses who dance for Miranda and Ferdinand in Act IV Scene 1. Prospero's power is also shown when he calls on spirits in the form of 'hunting dogs' to chase Caliban, Trinculo and Stephano away, also in Act IV Scene 1.

CHECKPOINT 15

In your opinion, is Prospero right to keep Ariel under his control?

But what sort of man is Prospero? Is it enough to say he is a magician who was once a ruler in Milan? On the one hand, Prospero shows a just and decent side. He assures Miranda when she is worried about the ship and its passengers in Act I Scene 2 that 'there is no soul – no, not so much perdition as an hair betid to any creature in the vessel' (lines 29–31). Prospero means that not a single hair on the head of any traveller has been harmed. He reminds Ariel that if it wasn't for him, Ariel would have remained locked up inside the trunk of a pine tree for ever. Prospero shows forgiveness to Alonso, Sebastian and even his brother Antonio for their past crimes against him. It also appears that, to begin with, Prospero treated Caliban well and showed him love.

But there is another side to Prospero. He can frighten and alarm, and his flashes of temper show a willingness to punish those who do not do as he commands. Ariel, who asks to be freed from being Prospero's servant, is told that if he complains again, Prospero will 'rend an oak' (I.2.294) and lock Ariel up in it for 'twelve winters' (line 296). When Caliban claims Prospero stole the island from him, Caliban is warned that if he does not carry out his duties he will be punished with 'old cramps' and 'aches' (lines 370–1). It is tempting to see Prospero as a slave-driver, willing to use violence to keep his servants in order. Prospero also allows Alonso to believe, if only for a few hours, that his only son has drowned, and almost seems to take pleasure in making Alonso wait to learn the truth.

For all this, at the end of the play, Prospero seems to be rather tired of the effort of ruling the island, and conjuring up spirits and magical powers in order to carry out his revenge. Prospero's speech, after he has presented the 'masque' to Ferdinand and Miranda in Act IV Scene 1, perhaps shows a man who has had enough of island life. He tells them, 'Our revels now are ended' (line 148), and that his 'old brain is troubled' (line 159).

When Prospero is finally faced with the opportunity to take revenge on his enemies, he says:

> Nobler reason 'gainst my fury
> Do I take part. The rarer action is
> In virtue than in vengeance. (V.1.26–8)

Thoughtfulness and sense have won out over anger. Prospero is suggesting that it is easy to give in to your emotions, but he will take the harder route of forgiveness.

Prospero leaves the island to resume his position as the rightful Duke of Milan and puts his magic behind him, his mission accomplished.

CHECKPOINT 16

In your opinion is Prospero basically a 'good' man? If not, why not?

 DID YOU KNOW?

The link between Prospero and an older, more thoughtful Shakespeare has been made before. In fact, Shakespeare was only fifty-four when he died – hardly an old man – though people did not live as long in those days.

CHECKPOINT 17

Why do you think Prospero decides to leave the island?

GLOSSARY

perdition harm
betid come to
virtue goodness
vengeance revenge

Wild
Comical
Poetic

CALIBAN

Caliban is a creature who was born on the island to the 'foul witch' Sycorax (I.2.9), before the play begins. He is seen throughout the play in many different ways. Firstly, as Prospero's 'slave', Caliban carries out physical duties (such as fetching wood) for him, and is treated rather like a working animal. We are told Prospero 'strok'st' him (I.2.34) when he first arrived on the island, and his knowledge of 'fresh springs, brine pits, barren place and fertile' (I.2.339) is like that of a native wild-dog or other hunting creature. However, we also see an almost human side: Caliban has been taught how to speak (by Miranda), and is capable of capturing the magic of the island as beautifully as any human in the play. Caliban's speech about the island's noises (III.2.132–40) and his knowledge of where to find a 'jay's nest', the 'nimble marmoset' and 'clustering filberts' (II.2.164–6) give real colour to the play. For all this, Caliban is also foolish and spiteful. He wishes to gain revenge on Prospero by murdering him, and has already tried to 'violate' Miranda (according to Prospero in Act I Scene 2). Caliban also becomes rather comic and idiotic when he meets up with Trinculo and Stephano in Act II Scene 2. In fact, their descriptions of Caliban as a 'moon-calf' (line 131) and 'a very shallow monster' (line 139) seem quite accurate by the end of the play.

Caliban begins the play with promises of rebellion against Prospero, and mistakenly believes Stephano and Trinculo will provide the means to carry out his revenge. By the end of the play, Caliban is back under Prospero's control, and says he will be 'wise hereafter' (V.1.294) – in other words, behave in a more intelligent way in the future.

Innocent
Loving
Strong willed

MIRANDA

Miranda came with her father, Prospero, when they first arrived on the island. Indeed, Miranda's whole knowledge of the world, until Ferdinand arrives, apart from some vague memories of her childhood nurses, is based on the island. Despite this, Miranda is shown to be caring and has a natural sense of what is right. She asks her father to calm the 'wild waters' of the storm (I.1.2). Miranda is presented as innocent, but with a teenager's natural attraction to a handsome young man.

Miranda tells her father that Ferdinand has a 'brave form' (I.2.415) and is a 'thing divine' (line 422) when she first sees him. Later, in the same scene, Miranda shows bravery as she stands up to her father, and begs him to be kind to Ferdinand, saying 'Make not too rash a trial of him' (lines 471–2). The sense of wonder Miranda feels when she sees Ferdinand is repeated again at the end of the play when Alonso and company appear. Miranda's words, 'O brave new world, that has such people in't' (V.1.184), show that she wants more than the island can offer and is ready for her new life back in Milan. Clearly intelligent, having taught Caliban to speak, Miranda shows no compassion for him in the play, and considers him a 'savage' (I.2.356), which is not surprising, perhaps, given what he tried to do to her.

ARIEL

Ariel is a spirit who can change shape, fly and become invisible. Originally released by Prospero from imprisonment by the witch Sycorax, Ariel has promised to serve him, 'be't to fly, to swim, to dive into the fire, to ride on the curled clouds' (I.2.190–1). Initially, Ariel shows unhappiness at having to do more work for Prospero, but once reminded of how Prospero helped him, and threatened with a punishment if he complains, he settles down to serve his master willingly. Ariel's reward is that once the current work is done, he will be free from Prospero's power.

Ariel is an active and almost permanent presence in the play, either at Prospero's side, or following the different groups of **characters** around the isle. Ariel conjures up the tempest for Prospero and scatters the voyagers all over the island. Ariel is on hand to warn them of danger, condemn them for their sins, and, finally, lead them to Prospero. In addition, Ariel feeds back information to his master, and even has time to help Prospero with his magical presentation for Ferdinand and Miranda.

As a 'character', Ariel, in his various forms, can be comical (when he imitates Trinculo's voice to create mischief in Act III Scene 2) but also stern and terrifying (when he appears as a harpy in Act III Scene 3). Prospero even wonders if Ariel, who is not mortal and is made of 'air' (V.1.21), can feel emotions like a human being. We

---

CHECKPOINT 18

Why do you think Prospero is worried at first about Miranda falling in love with Ferdinand?

Shape-changer
Spirit-like
Swift moving

GLOSSARY

brine salty water, or can mean simply the sea

barren lifeless

moon-calf a creature born deformed

hereafter from now on

brave handsome, strong and good

never know the answer to this because Ariel's prime **role** is to serve Prospero. By the end of the play, Prospero appears as close to him – perhaps closer – than he does to his own daughter, and his last words to Ariel are kind ones: 'Be free, and fare thou well!' (V.1.318).

FERDINAND

Princely
Brave
Good looking

Our first impression of Ferdinand is given by Ariel who describes his 'sighs' (I.2.222), presumably of sadness and despair, as he thinks about being alone on the island. Ferdinand himself says he has been sitting 'weeping' (line 393) when he first hears the magical music that draws him to Prospero's cave. Both these descriptions suggest a young man of heart-felt emotions, who is deeply affected by the apparent death of his father, Alonso.

However, despite his situation, Ferdinand shows bravery when he finally meets Prospero. Young and good looking, it is little surprise that Miranda falls in love with him. The feeling is clearly mutual and this perhaps encourages Ferdinand to stand up to Prospero. It is only Prospero's magical spell that prevents Ferdinand fighting for his freedom. Later, carrying out his work for Prospero, he puts up with hardship for Miranda's sake, saying, 'the mistress which I serve quickens what's dead, and makes my labours pleasures' (III.1.6–7). By this Ferdinand means that thinking about Miranda gives life to his feelings, which might otherwise have been depressed or deadened because of what he believes has happened to his father.

CHECKPOINT 19

How convinced are you by the love at first sight of Ferdinand and Miranda?

On the surface the two young people might seem to be mirror images of each other. However, when it comes to love, there are some subtle differences. Ferdinand is not entirely innocent, unlike Miranda, and admits to having 'liked several women' (line 43) but had always found them to have a 'defect' (line 44) of some sort. Ferdinand finds Miranda to be 'so perfect and so peerless' (line 47) that he knows she's *the one*. Despite Prospero's concerns about his motives, Ferdinand turns out to be decent and honourable and wins Miranda through his respectful treatment of her.

STEPHANO AND TRINCULO

Stephano, the butler, and his comic **side-kick** Trinculo, the king's jester, provide a good deal of the humour in the play, both **physical** and **verbal**. Stephano is arrogant, and believes he can become king of the island. Trinculo is happy to be his follower, but seems jealous of the friendship between Stephano and Caliban. He calls Caliban 'abominable', 'ridiculous' and 'scurvy' when they first meet in Act II Scene 2 (lines 150–4). Both end up looking foolish, having been distracted by the 'trash' (the flashy clothes hung on the line by Ariel and Prospero, in Act IV Scene 1) and therefore fail to carry out their plan to kill Prospero.

ALONSO

The King of Naples spends most of the play in a depressed daze, believing his son Ferdinand to be dead. Even Gonzalo's efforts to cheer him up do not work, and it seems that from the moment he is on the island Alonso's past crimes begin to catch up with him. When Ariel appears as a *'Harpy'* in Act III Scene 3 to condemn him, Antonio and Sebastian, it is Alonso who is the one most deeply affected by the experience. He says he has heard the thunder say Prospero's name, and that 'it did bass my trespass' (line 99). In other words, the thunder spoke of his guilt in a low voice. Alonso willingly allows Ferdinand to marry Miranda at the end of the play, and agrees to Prospero taking up his dukedom again.

CHECKPOINT 20

Who is gaining more out of the marriage of Ferdinand and Miranda? Prospero or Alonso?

ANTONIO AND SEBASTIAN

Antonio is Prospero's brother and the one who stole his dukedom from him twelve years before the play began. Sebastian is Alonso's brother. Both men are basically villains. They jointly plan to murder Alonso and Gonzalo for their own rewards. Despite being stopped by Ariel's warning to Gonzalo, and despite being aware that Prospero knows about their plans, Antonio and Sebastian do not seem to feel guilty. Another nasty side of them is shown when they make fun of loyal Gonzalo in Act II Scene 1, describing how long he takes to make a clever comment, saying it is like 'winding up the watch of his wit' (line 14). They do not appear to have changed or learned anything by the end of the play.

GONZALO

The old lord Gonzalo is a kind, loyal nobleman who serves Alonso, and was responsible for Prospero and Miranda surviving the open

EXAMINER'S SECRET

It is tempting to view Gonzalo as a physically weak, older man, who is rather slow to realise what is happening. But look at the *evidence*. In Act I Scene 1 he makes quite a rude joke about the ship being like an 'unstanched wench' (lines 44–5) (a loose woman) and Sebastian and Antonio do not try to murder him when he is awake.

DID YOU KNOW?

The word 'fathom' is a measure of depth and comes from an Old English word meaning 'outstretched arm' which is especially appropriate in this **verse**.

seas when they were first exiled from Milan. Gonzalo remains cheerful, being hopeful even during the storm in Act I Scene 1 when he says he can't imagine the Boatswain drowning. Gonzalo is still full of hope when they land on the island, although he fails to cheer up Alonso. He is the subject of cruel jokes from Antonio and Sebastian in Act II Scene 1, and does seem a little out-of-touch with reality. Gonzalo speaks of his dream kingdom, the 'commonwealth' (line 143) in which everyone is equal, but no one works! However, he is decent and is welcomed by Prospero as a 'noble friend … whose honour cannot be measured' (V.2.120–1).

IDEAS, THEMES AND ISSUES

MAGIC AND THE SUPERNATURAL

Supernatural and magical events take place on several occasions and for many reasons in the play. First and foremost they are Prospero's way of creating a situation in which he can get revenge on those who treated him so badly. This can be seen in the most striking event of the play – the tempest itself – which is like a show, or **production** that is 'performed' on Prospero's behalf by Ariel (I.2.194). But other, smaller, magical events take place, too, as when Prospero puts Miranda to sleep at the end of Act I Scene 2.

The magical and supernatural power of the play is mostly focused on Ariel, however. He carries out the tempest for Prospero, and then creates the tune/song that leads Ferdinand into Prospero's cell. The song itself is magical with its **alliteration** on the 'fs' – 'Full fathom five thy father lies' (lines 399–400) and sounds like a **tongue-twister** or spell. Later, in Act III Scene 2, Ariel outwits Caliban, Trinculo and Stephano by magically imitating Trinculo's voice as he watches the three **plotters**, and then conjures up the supernatural feast for Alonso and company (Act III Scene 3). Ariel also changes shape into a winged 'harpy', a **mythical** bird-like creature. Prospero himself takes a leading **role** in the 'majestic vision' (line 118) he creates for Ferdinand and Miranda in Act IV Scene 1. Ferdinand is wide-eyed in wonder at what he has seen, and asks Prospero if they are spirits. Prospero answers:

Spirits which by mine Art
I have from their confines called to enact
My present fancies. (lines 120–1)

Our final view of magical power is a positive one as Prospero, having released Alonso and company from the charmed circle (in Act V Scene 1), ends the play by promising everyone 'calm seas, auspicious gales' (line 314) for the journey home. Prospero will presumably conjure this up by his own magic.

It is important to remember that the island is strongly connected to the supernatural events. Prospero is already part-magician when he arrives (he has a 'magic cloak' after all!) but it is the island that makes the magic come alive. When Prospero leaves it, he breaks his staff (wand) for good. It is as if magic cannot exist outside the island.

POWER AND GOVERNMENT

There is much in the play about rulers and their subjects. Prospero, a ruler in Milan before the play begins, was overthrown by his brother, Antonio. Without this rebellion in the past there would be no story now. The island, of course, is like a kingdom, with Prospero as its supreme ruler, although Caliban mocks this idea telling him, 'I am all the subjects that you have' (I.2.342). This is as if Caliban was saying, 'You're not much of a ruler really if I'm your only subject.' Prospero probably realises the island is not like a real kingdom, which is why he chooses to leave in the end.

The play also asks lots of questions about what it means to be a ruler and how you should treat your people. Gonzalo, in Act II Scene 1, speaks at length about his 'commonwealth' and how it would be governed. He seems to be aiming for a form of paradise, which seems rather different from what the world is really like. On the island, after all, Caliban is treated like a slave by Prospero – but it is suggested he deserves it because of his behaviour to Miranda. Such a situation between master and servant would have no place in Gonzalo's perfect state.

So, bearing this in mind, is Prospero a *good* ruler? According to his own words he was loved by the people of Milan. However, he

CHECKPOINT 21

What power do you think Prospero's 'magic cloak' has?

 **EXAMINER'S SECRET**

The **theme** of magical power is important to the play, but if you are asked about it, try to think not just about what happens but also what it means for individual characters. In Prospero's long speech in Act V Scene 1, he says he has used magic for opening 'graves' and letting out the dead bodies (line 48), amongst other things.

GLOSSARY

auspicious favourable

subjects people under someone's rule

DID YOU KNOW?
The idea of someone being a ruler and studying magic was not unheard-of in Shakespeare's day. James I, who was on the throne when *The Tempest* was produced, wrote a book about demons and witches!

neglected many of his duties as ruler and passed them on to his brother, who used the opportunity to gain power. There is some evidence Prospero has learned from his mistakes. Whereas in Milan he spent too much time on 'secret studies' (I.2.77), on the island he seems to have a much better grasp of what is going on. His other two 'subjects' are, of course, Ariel and Miranda, but in both cases ruling them is not quite the same as ruling the people of Milan.

TEACHING AND LEARNING

The theme of learning is central to *The Tempest* in a number of ways. Firstly, we have the situation of Prospero before he arrived on the island. He confesses that he spent too much time 'neglecting worldly ends' (I.2.89) as a ruler in Milan, and 'bettering' (line 90) his mind – which is to say, when he should have been thinking about government, he was reading books! The message here seems to be that you cannot separate what you learn from life around you.

Later in the same **scene**, the theme is explored again through Caliban. We find out that when Prospero came to the island, Caliban learned from him – but also taught Prospero, in his own way. Caliban describes how Prospero taught him how to:

> … name the bigger light, and how the less
> That burn by day and night. And then I loved thee.

But also that Caliban himself showed Prospero:

> … all the qualities o'the isle,
> The fresh springs, brine pits, barren place and fertile.
> (lines 336–9)

Miranda also taught Caliban how to speak, but none of this learning seems to have changed him for the better. We have already discovered that Caliban tried to 'violate' (line 348) Miranda. What are we to make of all this? Miranda suggests that Caliban's 'race' (line 359) was basically savage and wild, and that whatever anyone tried, he would always be uncivilised. This touches upon the **debate** about which is more powerful: 'nature' (what you are like when you are born) or 'nurture' (how you change because of your upbringing). The play never completely answers the question. We see, for example, Alonso *learn* through his experience, and change as a person. By the end he feels guilt for his actions. On the other hand, Antonio, who we know behaved in a villainous way before the play had even begun, is still a villain at the end – and seems to have learned nothing from his experiences.

JUSTICE AND REVENGE

These related **themes** are central to the **plot**. It appears to be revenge Prospero wants when Alonso's ship passes the island, and a desire for justice that leads him to create a magical storm. But is revenge really the **motivation** for his actions? After all, Prospero realises it is luck that has brought the ship to him, and he needs to act immediately because if he doesn't, 'my fortunes will ever after droop' (I.2.183–4). Perhaps Prospero cannot carry out the revenge he would really like because he needs to escape from the island. To do this he needs the ship – and possibly he needs the king to be alive and on his side when he returns to Milan.

But, while **Fate** has delivered his enemies to him, Prospero can at least make them suffer. This is why he makes Alonso believe his son, Ferdinand, has drowned. This is why Prospero gets Ariel to offer Alonso and company delicious food in Act III Scene 3 and then snatches it away. This is why Prospero frightens them with thunder, with magical voices, and with charms that magically control their swords, and eventually drives them to a sort of madness.

The final scene (Act V Scene 1) brings together the idea of justice and revenge, and seems rather like a courtroom with the accused ready to face their sentences. Perhaps surprisingly, Prospero forgives them all, even Antonio, 'unnatural though thou art!' (line 79). Prospero gives them the justice which they failed to give him as Duke of Milan. And what about the other villains, Caliban, Stephano and Trinculo? They are punished in their own way – with Stephano a pathetic figure tortured with pain from Prospero's magic, and Caliban now aware of how stupid he was to trust two drunken fools.

> **CHECKPOINT 22**
>
> To what extent do you think luck (or 'Fate') is responsible for Prospero being able to succeed in his plans?

> **GLOSSARY**
> **the bigger light** the sun
> **the less** the moon

THE ISLAND

Whilst we cannot say the island itself is a '**theme**', it is worth mentioning because its presence is everywhere in the play – so perhaps it is a '**character**'. It is linked to all the other themes – and without it, there could be no revenge. It is the island's unique **setting** that enables Prospero to control and watch people. The island provides a wonderful setting for the supernatural events that occur, and it already has its own 'sounds and sweet airs' (III.2.132). The lack of buildings means that storms, rough landscape and so on can be used to great effect by Prospero. The island is linked to the theme of power and government because it is like a tiny version of a whole country with a ruler (Prospero) and his subjects (Ariel, Miranda and Caliban). It is even linked to learning – with Caliban teaching Prospero about it when he first arrived, and later trying to teach Stephano and Trinculo. But most of all the island provides an atmospheric **backdrop** to the play. There are countless references to its wildlife and its features – from the 'yellow sands' about which Ariel sings to Ferdinand, in Act I Scene 2, to the 'sharp furzes, pricking gorse, and thorns' (IV.1.180) that Ariel drags Caliban and company through. We hear about 'springs' and 'berries' from Caliban (Act II Scene 2) and later in the same scene about 'crabs', 'pig-nuts', 'marmosets', and 'scamels' (lines 162–7). But we also hear about 'bogs, fens, flats', 'hedgehogs' and 'adders' (II.2.2–13). It seems a strange mix of a southerly, tropical island and a colder, northern heap of rock and marsh. Perhaps this is part of the island's fascination.

> **CHECKPOINT 23**
>
> What image do you have of the island? Does it seem more tropical or northerly to you?

THE LANGUAGE OF THE TEXT

CHARACTERS AND HOW THEY SPEAK

The way **characters** speak – their *choice* of words, *how* they're spoken, and *when* and *why* they speak – all help us to decide how we see a particular person in a play. For example, Stephano first appears on stage in Act II Scene 2 carrying a bottle and singing a rude song about a girl called Kate! He repeats two **phrases**: first he calls his song a 'scurvy tune' and then says 'Here's my comfort' (lines 42–3). The fact that he enters singing a drunken song about a girl probably tells us quite a lot about his character. In the same way, the fact that he uses a word which is almost a swear word – 'scurvy', meaning 'bad', and not likely to be used by more noble characters – sets him apart from Prospero, Alonso and the others. 'Here's my comfort' is a reference to the bottle which allows him to 'comfort' himself in this rather strange place. Shakespeare has established Stephano in our minds by the way he speaks. When Stephano speaks in **prose**, as he does for the remainder of the **scene**, it is clear his **function** in the play is likely to be broadly humorous. It shows his 'level' in society. He is really no better than a servant – a butler.

Of course, we get quite different impressions of other characters from how they speak and what they say. Throughout the play, Prospero tends to speak in ways which fit with a former ruler and powerful man capable of creating magic. He speaks in **verse** – that is, lines of **poetry** – rather than the prose that Stephano uses. Look at how Prospero says to Miranda, 'What see'st thou else in the dark backward and abysm of time' (I.2.49–50) rather than simply saying, 'What else do you remember from the past?' He is speaking poetically of the past being like a deep, dark crater in which memories are buried.

Of course, *what* characters talk about is equally important. Stephano talks of drink and girls, and Prospero concerns himself with memories and plans. Caliban talks of revenge and the island, and Miranda talks of her worries over the shipwrecked crew, and later of her love for Ferdinand. People's characters are shown to us, therefore, through what they say and the **tone** of their speech – and, of course, by how much or how little they are given to say.

SONGS AND RHYMES

None of the more powerful noble characters sing, but Shakespeare does give songs to his spirits, servants and comic characters. Ariel uses a song, with invisible 'other spirit voices' in Act I Scene 2, to lead Ferdinand on to the stage. Ariel's first song talks of the 'wild waves' (line 379), which links it to the earlier storm. Ariel's second song talks directly to Ferdinand, telling him his father's 'bones are coral made' (line 400). This suggests his father's body, underwater,

 DID YOU KNOW?

Scurvy was a common disease amongst sailors who had been at sea a long time without fresh food, causing a lack of Vitamin C. The insult probably refers to the nasty appearance someone might have if they had scurvy.

 EXAMINER'S SECRET

Although it is *usually* true that more noble characters' lines are written in verse, and 'lower' or comic characters' in prose, look out for occasions when characters move between the two – for example, Caliban in Act III Scene 2. Do you think this might reflect the fact that while Caliban is often rude he can also speak beautifully?

GLOSSARY

crabs crab-apples

pig-nuts underground roots

scamels a type of sea-bird

DID YOU KNOW?

Similar spells and charms, with a regular **rhythm** and **rhyme**, occur in other Shakespeare plays, for example 'By the pricking of my thumbs / Something wicked this way comes', which is a couplet spoken by a witch in *Macbeth*. Check to see if it has the same rhythm as Ariel's rhyme in Act II Scene 1!

has disintegrated and joined up with the coral. Songs like these are important as they are part of the process of reminding people of their pain, their guilt, or their memories. This particular song is also magical and musical – and helps to create a strange atmosphere.

Ariel's next song, in Act II Scene 1, is much more focused and specific – it is used to wake Gonzalo and Alonso as they are about to be attacked, and sounds more like a spell designed to wake them from the sleep Ariel himself has put them into: 'If of life you keep a care, / Shake off slumber and beware' (lines 295–6).

Notice the regular rhythm and rhyme of this simple **couplet**, which is very like the charms and spells you might have heard in nursery rhymes and other **myths** and stories. Later, Stephano sings his drunken song, and is joined in singing at the end of Act II Scene 2 by Caliban, whose song is more like a rhythmic tribal chant – ''Ban! 'Ban! Ca–Caliban! Has a new master – Get a new man!' (lines 179–80) – fitting, perhaps, with the savage way Shakespeare may wish him to be seen. But it is Ariel, as the maker of music – like a Pied Piper that people follow – who has the greatest number of songs and rhymes. Even his 'ordinary' speech is peppered with language that makes it more like singing than speaking, so that in Act IV Scene 1, when Prospero asks Ariel to organise a show for Ferdinand and Miranda, Ariel tells him:

> Before you can say, 'Come' and 'Go',
> And breathe twice, and cry, 'So, so',
> Each one tripping on his toe,
> Will be here with mop and mow. (lines 44–7)

Shakespeare needs to make sure Ariel is seen as different, as playful and impish, and the language helps him do that.

IMAGERY

Imagery is the use of language to create strong pictures in the reader's, or listener's, mind. These give power to the emotions being expressed, or explain more specifically how someone feels or behaves. Often, but not always, these images are part of **similes** or **metaphors**. Similes are when something is described as being *like* something else. For example, Gonzalo uses a simile to describe how

Alonso, Antonio and Sebastian are slowly beginning to feel the guilt of their crimes, and says it is 'like poison given to work a great time after, now 'gins to bite the spirits' (III.3.105–6). In other words, their guilt is like a slow-acting poison.

A metaphor describes something as if it really *is* something else. A metaphor is even more powerful – and is regularly used for effect in the play. For example, early in the play Prospero describes how his brother, Antonio, had cleverly kept close to him, slowly taking his power. Prospero says Antonio was 'the ivy which hid my princely trunk, and sucked the verdure out on't' (I.2.86–7). In other words, a handsome tree which is smothered in ivy that sucks out its life.

Of course, images can simply be clear, vivid descriptions that create atmospheric pictures in the **audience**'s mind. For example, when Prospero describes how he has used natural forces to assist him, he speaks about 'hills, brooks, standing lakes and groves', 'the mutinous winds', 'the green sea and the azured vault', and the 'dread rattling thunder' (V.1.33–44). This gives a picture of a calm, picture-postcard landscape in one breath, and nature in uproar in the next.

Perhaps the most powerful image which runs through the play is the idea of the world as we know it – our lives – being a vision or a dream. When Prospero tells Ferdinand and Miranda in Act IV Scene 1 that their 'revels' (games or entertainments) are at an end, he goes on to say that the 'cloud-capp'd towers, the gorgeous palaces, the solemn temples' (lines 152–3) will all fade away, just like the show he has just presented to them. Prospero adds that as people they are all 'such stuff as dreams are made on' (lines 156–7), as if to say that their lives are almost unreal, like dreams that will dissolve when sleep ends.

INSULTS

The Tempest has many scenes in which characters, for one reason or another, speak cruelly or in an insulting way. We see this even in the very first scene of the play when Sebastian and Antonio shout curses at the Boatswain who has criticised them for not helping save the ship. Sebastian calls him, 'a bawling, blasphemous, incharitable

EXAMINER'S SECRET

It is actually quite easy to 'spot' a simile or metaphor, and even to explain it, but your response will look even better if you are able to write about the *suitability* of the image. For example, 'poison' is a very good comparison for 'guilt' because of the way both might make you suffer and feel pain.

GLOSSARY
blasphemous rude about God or other sacred beings

dog!' (I.1.38–9), whilst Antonio calls him, 'a whoreson, insolent noise-maker!' (line 41). This way of speaking is continued even by Prospero who calls Ariel a 'malignant thing' (I.2.258) when he forgets how Prospero had helped him. Later in the same scene Prospero calls Caliban a 'poisonous slave' (line 320) and 'hag-seed' (line 367). However, more noticeable than all these examples are the insults exchanged between Stephano, Trinculo and Caliban. Trinculo, in particular, seems to really dislike Caliban, calling him from the start, 'a most scurvy monster' (II.2.150), an 'abominable monster' (line 153), and later, a 'debauched fish' (III.2.25), although Caliban finally starts to answer Trinculo back, calling him in turn 'a pied ninny' and a 'scurvy patch' (line 62)!

The effect of this is to give a rough energy both to the comic scenes, but also to the meetings between Prospero and Caliban, and Prospero and Ariel. In contrast to their straightforward rudeness, Sebastian and Antonio's insults towards Gonzalo once they are all on the island are much more devious and mocking. This fits in with their cunning and rather nasty personalities. Look at how they sarcastically congratulate Gonzalo in Act II Scene 1 when he is describing how he would rule the island if it was his:

Sebastian:	Save his Majesty!
Antonio:	Long live Gonzalo! (lines 163–4)

THE TEXT IN PERFORMANCE

SETTING

The play takes place exclusively on the island, apart from Act I Scene 1, which occurs on the storm-hit ship. However, despite the fact that there are quite a few **stage directions** about movements, appearances, behaviour and so on, we are told next to nothing about the **setting** in the stage directions at the start of each **scene**. The action either takes place in front of Prospero's cave, or on *'another part of the island'*. We know from Act I Scene 2 that Ariel has placed the ship in a 'deep nook' (line 227), which is like a cove or inlet. All our evidence for the setting comes from the atmospheric descriptions provided by the **characters** (see **Themes: The island**).

We are told of the various animals and fish that can be caught; there are references to trees (oaks, pines, cedars), types of landscape (marshes, fens, lakes); and there is 'yellow sand' (I.1.375) – as well as the magical sounds of the isle. But we do not know where any of these things are. If you were asked to draw a map of the island, you would not be able to say *where* the lake was, or what *part* had forests of oaks and pines. The island, then, for all the details we are given, is what we – the **audience** – make it. Or perhaps what the **director** and the actors make it.

So, how should a director **interpret** the island and what it is like? And what about Prospero's cell, which he describes as humble, yet is obviously more comfortable than the 'hard rock' (I.2.344) that Caliban is kept in – unless they are one and the same? The cell has room for a chess-board, and in Act IV Scene 1 Prospero and Ariel place garments on the line that must be quite fashionable, as Stephano and Trinculo try to steal them. Have these clothes been brought all the way from Milan? It is difficult to picture a cave in which a magician lives with his daughter filled with the things they brought with them from their old lives.

In the end, the strange mix of detailed information about the island's features and forms, and lack of specific *locations* are what make this a perfect play to interpret. If you write about it in your test, you can bring together the evidence with your own personal vision of the island.

CHALLENGES

The Tempest is a wonderful play to perform, but of course presents many challenges to directors. Amongst these are how you can make a storm seem real on stage (Act I Scene 1); how you should dress a spirit, like Ariel; how you can bring 'hunting dogs' on to the stage (Act IV Scene 1); and how you can make spells and charms convincing. But these are not the only challenges. Some are to do with the **text** itself. For example, whilst there is no problem holding an audience's attention with the storm in Act I Scene 1, the long section where Prospero explains what happened before he and Miranda came to the island is more difficult. **Productions** in the past have sometimes left out this scene altogether and found a

---

CHECKPOINT 24

Do you have a view about how large the island is? What evidence is there for it being relatively small?

CHECKPOINT 25

How different do you think the play would be if the first scene had been with Prospero and Miranda talking about the storm, rather than the storm itself?

 DID YOU KNOW?

The sound effects of the storm in the opening scene mean that some directors have worried that no one can hear a word of what anyone is saying!

GLOSSARY

malignant very harmful

pied multi-coloured, or 'like a magpie'

different way of showing it, or have illustrated what Prospero recounts with mime, or images projected on to the back of the stage. An audience in Shakespeare's day would not have found it boring – they would have enjoyed the story-telling and the filling-in of information. We have less concentration as audiences nowadays!

OPPORTUNITIES

One of the strengths of the play is its variety. Three – sometimes four (if you count Ferdinand and Miranda) – sets of people have their own stories. This makes it interesting, rather like a modern day soap opera switching between a funny scene in a pub (Caliban, Stephano and Trinculo?) to a love scene in a living-room (Ferdinand and Miranda?) to a criminal meeting in a night-club (Sebastian and Antonio?). But part of this strength is the variety of characters too – we have a magician, a king, a spirit, a prince, a pretty daughter, a monster, a clown, two villains and dancing goddesses. Something for everyone, perhaps?

EXAMINER'S SECRET

When thinking about how a particular character might look or behave, it can be useful to gather together snapshots of people's faces, clothing, etc. from colour magazines, until you find the 'right' look for a character. This is actually something some **directors** do when working out how to **interpret** the play.

But how do you play these parts? What *sort* of monster is Caliban and what should the actor who plays him aim to make the audience *feel*? Is Caliban a savage monster who roars and acts like a caveman? Or is he like a **tragic** child, searching for a master who will genuinely care for him? The challenges for the actor are going to be how to switch from the wild creature who freely admits to having wanted to 'violate' Miranda (I.2.348), to the almost child-like 'moon-calf' who speaks so beautifully of the island in Act III Scene 2 (lines 132–40). Look, in particular, at Caliban's first major speech to Prospero and Miranda in Act I Scene 2 (lines 331–44), and consider how his language moves from defiance ('This island's mine') to reflection ('Thou strok'st me') to anger ('Cursed be I that did so!') and so on. How could this be shown through gestures and voice? Perhaps by shaking a fist, roaring out loud, or half-sobbing?

STAGING

Despite the lack of detail about the scenes and where they take place, there are more individual stage directions about movements, gestures and how things look in *The Tempest* than we would normally find in Shakespeare's plays. It can be useful to consider them when thinking about how the play might be performed as quite a lot of detail is provided for the director or actor/actress to use.

When Ariel describes how he has left Ferdinand sitting with his arms in a 'sad knot' (I.2.224), for example, we are told that Ariel himself demonstrates this (*'He folds his arms'*). This could be shown again when we see Ferdinand. Perhaps he could sink to the ground and make the same shape as Ariel has suggested? Later when Ferdinand, in Act III Scene 1, is collecting the logs, there are little reminders in the text (*'He picks up the log again'*, *'Putting down the log'*), which help get across the sense that while Ferdinand speaks between lines 14 and 35, he is still physically active and busy. This is extremely useful for directors or actors, as this scene, essentially a love scene, could be dull to watch. The constant moving of the logs makes it clear that Prospero really has imprisoned Ferdinand and is making him suffer for his love of his daughter, for the time being at least.

Even greater detail is given in Act V Scene 1 when Alonso and company are brought on to the stage. The stage directions here are very clear, from the *'solemn music'* that is playing, through the *'magic circle'* marked by Prospero on the ground, to the *'maddened'* state of the men who enter and stand *'under the power of his spell'*.

It is easy to get a sense of the look and atmosphere of this scene, but questions remain. If they are in the magic circle, are they themselves standing in a circle formation, or are they in a line? What difference would that make to how the audience view them? Where does Prospero stand as he speaks to them one by one, in their trance? Is he behind them, speaking over their shoulders, whispering into their ears? Or is he facing them, glaring at these men who have betrayed him? There are many decisions to make, and the voice that Prospero uses, whether gentle, mocking, angry or sad, will affect how we see him and those present.

 DID YOU KNOW?

Despite there being few stage directions in Shakespeare's plays, some have become almost as famous as the spoken lines. One of the most well known is from *The Winter's Tale* in which one poor character leaves the stage following the instruction *'Exit, pursued by a bear'*. He is never seen again!

CHECKPOINT 26

How do you think Shakespeare meant Alonso and company to look when he says they are led on to the stage in a *'maddened'* state?

STRUCTURE

Tension and drama

The play is taken up with a number of questions to which we, the **audience**, want to know the answers. Firstly, what will Prospero do when he finally brings together all his enemies and reveals that he is alive? This is a constant question throughout and is made interesting by Prospero's own unexpected changes in behaviour, moving from quiet kindness to violent punishment. How will he behave towards his enemies?

Then there is the question of Ferdinand and Miranda, and what will happen to them. As an audience we can perhaps see that joining them in marriage will be a 'neat' way of creating peace and harmony, but audiences in Shakespeare's day would have been aware that young love does not always end in happiness.

There are two other plot-lines which create tension and drama. Perhaps the most interesting is Sebastian and Antonio's plan to murder Alonso and Gonzalo. These two men are real villains, so we have no difficulty believing that when they raise their swords in Act II Scene 1 they are capable of murder. It is a very dramatic moment as, just in time, Ariel wakes Gonzalo and warns him. It is perhaps less believable that Caliban and his two drunken companions, Stephano and Trinculo, will succeed in their plot, but it is still exciting when we wait to find out how they are dealt with. We enjoy Ariel's trickery as they get closer to Prospero's cell. Caliban's desire to kill Prospero, however, seems quite genuine, so who knows what might happen?

Stories within stories

Although there are some **contradictions**, it is generally assumed that the play takes place within the course of less than a day. However, this does create its own difficulties. Everything about the characters' lives and backgrounds has to be shown in the present moment, and this is why there are so many 'stories within stories'. In the course of the play, we learn about the voyage Alonso was on and where he was going. We find out how Prospero came to be on the island and we find out how Ariel came to be Prospero's servant.

EXAMINER'S SECRET

It is good to look at the role **characters** play in the **plot**, and not just see them as individual personalities. The romance between Ferdinand and Miranda is important because Prospero uses it to keep Ferdinand away from Alonso, and then eventually to bring his old enemy to him.

CHECKPOINT 27

What do you think are the problems of including the sequence in Act IV Scene 1 when the goddesses/spirits perform for Ferdinand and Miranda?

We learn about Caliban's parentage, and how he came to be Prospero's slave. Another story, of a kind, is the one presented to Ferdinand and Miranda in Act IV Scene 1 by Prospero, when spirits perform as the goddesses Iris, Ceres and Juno. This is almost like an advertising break or musical **interlude** in the middle of the main film! It doesn't add anything in terms of the plot, but creates variety and atmosphere. Finally, there are the stories we never see, but which we wonder about as the play draws to a close – what will happen to Caliban when Prospero and Miranda leave? What will life be like for everyone back in the 'real world'? What will Ariel become, and where will he go, when Prospero frees him?

These may seem unimportant, but when you write about the play – especially the ending – it is useful to consider how 'finished' it is. Is everything complete? Are all the ends tied up? Is everything neatly resolved, or do some questions still remain?

> **CHECKPOINT 28**
>
> Typically, in Shakespeare's plays, the last scene or act is used to reveal the truth about people or situations. What **revelations** are there in the last part of Act V from the moment Alonso and company wake up?

Now take a break!

PART FOUR

THE TEST

UNDERSTANDING THE QUESTION

EXAMINER'S SECRET

You will be given 45 minutes to answer your question. You are advised to spend 5 minutes planning and 5 minutes checking your answer. This means that you have 35 minutes to write your essay. If you plan carefully and know the play, this is plenty of time!

There are **four** different types of question that the examiner can ask you about *The Tempest*. There are questions about:

1) Character and motivation: This means the examiner will ask you about a particular **character**. You will need to explain the reason the character is behaving in the way he or she is. You will be expected to look at the clues that Shakespeare gives us and understand how the chosen character's behaviour may be viewed by different characters. You will also be expected to understand how the character's behaviour may change over time. It is likely that you will be asked about the main characters of Prospero, Caliban, Ariel, Ferdinand and Miranda, but the examiner may also ask you about Gonzalo, Alonso, Sebastian, Antonio, Stephano or even Trinculo.

2) Ideas, themes and issues: This means the examiner will ask you about one of the things that Shakespeare seems to be talking about in his play. You will be expected to understand what Shakespeare has to say about this idea, **theme** or issue, and you will need to provide **evidence** from the play to back up what you say. Themes such as justice and revenge, and magic are likely to be popular questions here but the examiner may also ask you about other themes or ideas, such as the role of learning, or what we find out about power and government.

3) The language of the text: This means the examiner will ask you about Shakespeare's choice of language, and the techniques he uses. You will be expected to pick out important examples and then talk about the effect these are meant to have on the **audience**. When studying *The Tempest,* you might be asked to discuss Shakespeare's references to songs and music: for example, the way in which songs are used as spells and charms. Or you might be asked about Shakespeare's use of **imagery**: how a magical vision or dream is used to describe reality.

4) The text in performance: This means the examiner will ask you about the kind of decisions that you would make if you were directing a **performance** of the play. You need to think about what sort of **impact** these decisions would have on the audience. You could describe an actor using a certain type of facial expression or tone of voice. You will need to base your ideas about a character's appearance or the mood of a **scene** on what you find in the play itself. With *The Tempest* you could be asked to direct an actor playing Caliban (for example) through two extracts, explaining how the actor should show his reactions and giving reasons for your suggestions.

In class, you will have been preparing two or three sections of the play. In the test, the examiner will have chosen two short extracts from these sections for you to write about.

This means that as long as you can understand the question you will know exactly what the examiner is expecting to see in the answer that you give. For instance:

Act I Scene 2 lines 322–75

Act III Scene 2 lines 85–142

What contrasting impressions do we get of Caliban in both these extracts?

What are the **key words** in this question? The name **Caliban** tells us whom we are to focus on but also makes it clear to us that we are answering a **character and motivation** question. This is also given away by the word **impression.** This means we are expected to look at the way Caliban behaves, and think about how this could be viewed by the different audiences of the play and the other characters on the stage. The examiner has given us some extra help by including the word **contrasting** in the question. The examiner is suggesting that we build an argument, using the words from the play, to help us show that Caliban has very different aspects to his character in these extracts. However, it is important to look at the use of the words **in both.** The examiner is suggesting that even *within* each extract, Caliban shows different sides of his character.

EXAMINER'S SECRET

No matter what type of question you are answering, you will need to be able to talk about the language Shakespeare uses. You might also find that it is useful to talk about a particular theme when discussing a character.

You would need to discuss this in your answer. When it comes to your test, the extracts will be provided in the test booklet. This means that you can read these over before you begin to plan your answer.

LOOKING AT THE EVIDENCE

It is very important to make sure your answer is closely linked to what happens in the extracts you have been given. Let's imagine we are still trying to answer the question about Caliban. When discussing Caliban it could be easy to get carried away and talk about his arguments with Trinculo, and his adoration of Stephano when he first sees him. However, these things do not take place in the part of the play that the examiner has asked us to talk about. Therefore, it is better to find **evidence** of Caliban's **character** in the extracts we have been given, and then think through our ideas.

EXAMINER'S SECRET

Finding evidence about a character's behaviour and **motivations** can be simplified into the **four whats: what** the character *says*; **what** the character *does*; **what** *others say* about the character; **what** *others do* (to the character, or in response to them).

What evidence do we have?

Act I Scene 2 lines 322–75

- Caliban enters cursing Prospero and Miranda.

- Caliban talks about his past relationship with them both.

- Prospero and Miranda give their own versions of what Caliban is like and how he has acted in the past.

Act III Scene 2 lines 85–142

- Caliban describes how he, Stephano and Trinculo could kill Prospero.

- The three appear happy with their plans and sing and dance.

- Strange music plays and Caliban explains the island's magical charm.

Once we have found the evidence from the extracts we can see that Caliban feels resentment at how he has been treated by Prospero and Miranda. He is full of hate and spite. Prospero and Miranda in turn give us reasons why they treat him as they do, which may create a different impression of Caliban. In the second extract, we see that Caliban is capable of following up on the anger he feels. His plan to murder Prospero is evidence of this. At the same time, however, Caliban's beautiful speech about the island suggests he has a more human, poetic side.

By looking at the evidence we have found an answer to our question. We have also made sure that this evidence is from the correct part of the play.

> **CHECKPOINT 29**
> Do you agree that there are contrasting ways of viewing Caliban, or do you think he is less complicated than that?

WRITING YOUR ANSWER

The examiner is asking you to write about **two extracts** from the set scenes. You are asked to do this because the examiner wants to see if you can follow **developments** between the scenes, comment on **contrasts** and **comparisons**, or consider the same issues at different moments. Looking at different sections should also encourage you to come up with a **variety** of ideas. A good way to approach these questions is to look at each extract, one at a time. However, you must make connections between the extracts, using **connectives** to help you.

It is important that you **structure** your answer well. This means thinking about what you will write at the start, the middle and the end of your essay. Although you won't have much time to plan your answer in the test, as soon as you read a question you should start thinking about how best to tackle it. A good structure will help you make your points clearly and allow your **argument** to flow.

A POSSIBLE STRUCTURE
The answer to the question about Caliban may look something like this:

1) Introduction
Introduce what part Caliban has in the play. *Briefly* say what part Caliban plays in the two extracts.

2) Section 1: Act I Scene 2 lines 322–75

- We get the impression that Caliban has been badly treated by Prospero, and can be viewed sympathetically.

- Caliban describes how he was the first inhabitant of the island and how Prospero took it from him – does this add to our sympathy?

- We learn from Prospero and Miranda that Caliban tried to 'violate' Miranda despite her apparent kindness.

3) Section 2: Act III Scene 2 lines 85–142

- Caliban's resentment and desire for revenge are shown in his vivid plan to murder Prospero.

- Caliban appears rather comical as he starts to sing and dance with Stephano and Trinculo.

- Caliban is not afraid of the strange music which is playing; he seems almost like a child when he describes the island's magical charm.

EXAMINER'S SECRET

Try not to repeat yourself in your essay. If you make a point about the first extract and need to say something similar about the second extract, try to find a new way of saying it. This will make your essay more interesting.

4) Conclusion

Answer the question: What are the contrasting impressions of Caliban in the two extracts?

This answer is split into four sections. The aims of an introduction and a conclusion are the same no matter what the question. The introduction aims to say something about the **key words** in the question. It also aims to say briefly how both the extracts are linked to those key words. The conclusion always aims to answer the question in brief. The middle two sections look at the extracts closely. Look at how the bullet points directly answer the question. It is important that each bullet point becomes one paragraph in your essay. Following this structure you would write at least six short paragraphs, plus an introduction and conclusion.

ADDING DETAIL TO YOUR STRUCTURE

Of course, your basic structure is not the essay itself. You need to add three important things when writing your answer:

1. Quotations which are relevant to the points you want to make

2. Detailed explanations of your points

3. Links between the two extracts

For example, a suitable quotation is needed for the following point:

● We get the impression that Caliban has been badly treated by Prospero, and can be viewed sympathetically.

The quotation could be:

'When thou cam'st first
Thou strok'st me, and made much of me ...'

The detailed explanation could be:

Caliban is recalling how Prospero treated him at 'first' when he arrived on the island. Caliban's description of how Prospero stroked him, and 'made much' of him, make Caliban seem like a domesticated pet, or a small child, and might make us feel sympathy for him. The use of the word 'first' reminds us that this is all in the past, and things are very different now.

The link to the next extract could be:

Although we have been given some evidence of Caliban's kinder, gentler side in the first extract, most of the second extract is taken up with plans to murder Prospero. However, this rather more humane and thoughtful side of Caliban does reappear in Act III Scene 2 when he describes the 'sounds and sweet airs' of the island.

This can be done for **every** bullet point in your structure. In other words, for each paragraph you need to:

● make your point

● add supporting quotation(s)

● add some detailed explanation

● add a link to the other extract (and sometimes links to elsewhere in the play)

EXAMINER'S SECRET

Finding interesting angles on the play and relationships within it will make your writing stand out. For example, much of the play is about family relationships, especially between brothers and between fathers and children. But what about Miranda and Caliban? Firstly, they are like brother and sister – both brought up by Prospero. Secondly, Miranda acts almost like a mother, teaching Caliban to speak. Finally, Caliban obviously desires Miranda too – hence his attack on her. Exploring these ideas can lead to some real insight into the play.

PLANNING IN THE TEST ITSELF

Of course, in the actual test, you will not be able to write out the full structure as we have done above. You will need to reduce your structure to a **basic plan** as follows:

Introduction

● Caliban's part in the play.

● The part he plays in the two extracts.

Extract 1

● Caliban is an angry slave full of curses.

● He is treated badly by Prospero.

● Prospero took the island from Caliban.

● Prospero and Miranda's views – Caliban is savage and violent.

Extract 2

● Caliban is a plotter and would-be murderer.

● Caliban is a clown/fool.

● Caliban is a gentle native of the island – he is poetic, and so on.

Conclusion

Impressions of Caliban are full of contradictions: he is savage but human, rough but poetic, sympathetic but capable of planning murder.

In addition, you may want to note down quickly a few key words from the extracts, which you plan to use to support your ideas.

EXAMINER'S SECRET

Sometimes a famous **quotation**, **phrase** or line you have spent a lot of time studying will appear in your set extracts. But be careful! Only refer to it if it helps you answer the question.

HOW TO USE QUOTATIONS

CHOOSING THE RIGHT QUOTATION

As you read through the test booklet you might have made notes, on a separate sheet, of words from the play that look useful for your essay. In writing your essay, you need to find a way of inserting these words, called quotations, into your writing. In order to choose good quotations you first need to know how to use them.

Quotations can be used in different ways:

- to prove what you are saying is true

- to enable you to make an interesting and detailed point about a character, theme, etc.

You can use both these types of quotations in your essay. However, finding quotations that prove what you are saying is true *and* allow you to make interesting and original points will get you the highest level in the test. Therefore, when you are choosing a quotation you need to ask yourself (a) does it prove my point and (b) what can I say about it?

HOW TO PUT THE QUOTATIONS IN YOUR ESSAY

The examiner asks you to **select** and **retrieve** information from the play. You are also expected to be able to use quotations successfully, including them at the right points in your essay. There are two ways of doing this:

1. You can stop your paragraph and then write out the short part of the play that you have selected.

2. You can take Shakespeare's words and make them flow into your sentence. This is called **embedding** the quotation.

Method 1: Separated quotations

When you want to discuss a quotation in detail you may want to make your point, drop down a line, and then write in your quotation. This method of using quotations is shown below:

> Caliban talks about how Prospero mistreated him, having at first appeared to be kind. Caliban claims that he is the rightful ruler of the island:

> > This island's mine, by Sycorax my mother,
> > Which thou tak'st from me.

> Caliban talks about the lack of fairness in Prospero's actions,

reminding Prospero that he was born on the island, and that Prospero stole it from him: 'thou tak'st from me'. Caliban's statement, 'This island's mine', makes it clear that he feels he has the right to govern it. The impression created here is of a creature who feels he has been treated unjustly, and this makes us feel some sympathy for his situation. The themes of justice and government are both important here.

Look at how this method clearly separates the quotation so that you can comment on Shakespeare's language, and what it says about the character and his attitude. By moving down a line you are making it clear to the examiner that this is a quotation you are going to say something important about.

Method 2: Embedding

Sometimes, however, you may want to use **quotations** from the play as a way of illustrating your points clearly without breaking the flow of your paragraph. Inserting, or embedding, small quotations into your sentences will show the examiner that you are taking your ideas directly from the play. Look at how this is done below:

EXAMINER'S SECRET

You can use lists of single words from the play to prove a point and emphasise what you want to say. For example, you might say, 'It's difficult not to feel sympathy for Caliban in this scene: at various times he is called "hag-seed", "slave", and "malice".'

In Act I Scene 2, Caliban enters cursing Prospero and Miranda. He wishes for a 'wicked dew' to settle on them, and a symbol of evil, 'a raven's feather', to be blown on to them from an 'unwholesome fen'. These references link Caliban to his mother, who was a witch. They make us think of spells or curses she might have placed on Prospero and Miranda herself to punish them for mistreating her son. Unfortunately for Caliban, he does not have these powers and can only defend himself with words. Prospero, however, has his own magic powers that are much greater, which is why Caliban can be enslaved by him.

This answer is excellent because intelligent points are made using short quotations. Using quotations in this way has the advantage of showing the examiner that you can retrieve information from the text whilst at the same time allowing your essay to flow.

IMPROVE YOUR LEVEL

In the Key Stage 3 Reading test, there are four possible grades, or levels, that you can achieve: Levels 4–7. It is important that you know what it is that the questions expect from you, and how you can achieve the level you deserve.

A GENERAL GUIDE

Level 5 will be given when:

- You have focused clearly on the question.

- You show a generally clear understanding of the main points.

- You have used well-chosen evidence or quotations.

- You have developed some of your arguments.

- Your general writing is clear, if not always as **fluent** as it could be.

Higher levels will be given when:

- You have focused on the question clearly throughout.

- Your evidence and quotations are entirely suitable.

- You have suggested alternative, or original, ideas.

- You have shown **insight** (looked beyond the obvious).

- Your general writing is fluent and **coherent** (reads very well).

So, what would this actually mean if you were answering a question on *The Tempest*?

1) Character and motivation

Character questions are likely to ask you about the impression you get of a character because of the way they behave or the things they say. For instance, the examiner may ask you about the impression you get of Prospero in Act IV Scene 1 lines 139–93 and Act V Scene 1 lines 33–87. You might look at how in the first extract, when Prospero ends the show he has put on for Ferdinand and Miranda,

EXAMINER'S SECRET
Even though you know the whole of the play it is very important that you *focus* on the extracts mentioned in the question.

DID YOU KNOW?

Actors and directors often use the word 'motivation' to understand what a character wants at a particular point in the play. The answer can be something simple, such as 'Caliban wants to eat food', or more emotional, such as 'Prospero wants to make Miranda understand how they came to be on the island'.

EXAMINER'S SECRET

Often questions in the test will relate to a **character's** *development* between two scenes. This doesn't always mean that the character learns or improves. Sometimes, it might be asking how he or she gets worse.

he seems 'in some passion that works him strongly'. Prospero suggests that life is rather meaningless and is just a dream. However, in the second extract Prospero is much calmer. A Level 5 answer would conclude that in Act V Prospero seems to have recovered his self-control and is ready to pass judgement on – and give forgiveness to – his enemies. What else would you have to do to improve your level?

● A higher level answer would use **less obvious examples**, perhaps mentioning how it is Caliban's plot that seems to make Prospero angry. Prospero says how, until now, he had forgotten 'that foul conspiracy of the beast Caliban'. It seems strange that this is what concerns him most, rather than the much bigger betrayal by Alonso and Antonio.

● A higher level answer would also offer **an alternative** to the view that Prospero has regained his calm when he speaks to his enemies as they stand in front of him. For example, Prospero refers to Antonio being 'flesh and blood' yet 'unnatural', as if he still can't quite believe Antonio's evil nature.

2) Ideas, themes and issues

Ideas, **themes** and issues questions will ask you to talk about one of the things that Shakespeare has been concerned about in the play. You will be expected to explore the **evidence** and the different ways of looking at this evidence. For instance, the examiner may ask you about justice and revenge in two different extracts, one of which is Act III Scene 3 lines 53–102. You may make the point that Ariel directly states that Alonso, Antonio and Sebastian are 'three men of Sin'. A Level 5 answer would be able to understand that Ariel is speaking like a judge, or a prosecutor in a trial.

● A higher level answer would **explore** the power of the **language** and how it follows the idea of crime and punishment. Ariel tells Alonso that 'lingering perdition' will 'step by step attend you', a vivid use of language that makes it clear that Alonso will be pursued wherever he goes by ruin and guilt. Ariel means that Alonso will spend his life in shame and regret.

● A higher level answer would discuss this idea **fluently**.

3) The language of the text

Language questions will ask you to look at they way that Shakespeare uses language in two extracts and the effect this has on the **audience**. For instance, you may be asked to talk about the importance of songs and music in Act I Scene 2 lines 376–421 and Act II Scene 1 lines 282–319. You could make the point that Shakespeare uses songs and music in different ways, sometimes to warn people, and at other times to mislead or deceive them. A Level 5 answer would mention that Ariel is the chief maker of songs and music.

- A higher level answer would **develop** this idea, noticing that Ariel's manner of speaking and choice of **rhythm** and regular **rhyme** links him to charms and spells in fairy tales and **myths**.

- A higher level answer would also look to explore in more **subtle** detail how the various examples are different in both **tone** and effect – for example, focusing on the **alliteration** of 'Full fathom five' and 'wild waves whist' which seem almost musical in their tone, and the more commanding 'If of life you keep a care / Shake off slumber and beware!'

4) The text in performance

Performance questions will ask you to think like a **director** and consider how the play should be performed. They will ask you to focus on two extracts and explore how they would be performed differently. For instance, they may ask you to look at the performance of Prospero in Act I Scene 2 when he speaks to Ariel and then Caliban, and compare it with his performance at the end of Act V Scene 1 after Alonso and company awake. A Level 5 answer would point out Prospero's stern, powerful and almost cruel manner in the first extract. This would **contrast** with his kinder, more forgiving manner in the second extract. A higher level answer would need to be much more **developed**:

- It would show **insight** into Prospero's character and recognise that he is driven to anger by Caliban and Ariel 'rebelling' against his authority. It would point out that the two arguments Prospero has might show someone who is capable of violence as

EXAMINER'S SECRET

It is sometimes useful to think of ideas, themes and issues as repeating songs or tunes that keep on coming back within the play. In this way, the 'tune' of justice – how someone should be treated as a result of their actions – keeps on 'being heard' throughout the play.

CHECKPOINT 30

Is there any particular gesture or movement Prospero could make in the two extracts mentioned that would show a change in him from the stern master of Act I Scene 2 to the forgiving, older man at the end of Act V Scene 1?

well as love. This would need to be reflected in careful, detailed references to gesture, movement and tone of voice.

EXAMINER'S SECRET

It is important to offer alternative points of view in questions. There is often more than one way to view the same piece of evidence.

- A higher level answer would also explore the **function** of these extracts. It would do this by exploring how both extracts show Prospero as ruler of his kingdom. The first shows him having problems with his 'subjects', but also using the scene to fill in the background to the play as Prospero attempts to put all his plans in place. The second, on the other hand, shows Prospero giving his judgement, almost without passion or anger. He is trying to 'tie up' all the loose ends. These two elements would need to be shown when describing how Prospero behaves.

FURTHER QUESTIONS

Here are eight sample test questions you can use for practice. Try answering each one using the advice provided in these Notes. You could spend 5 minutes writing a short plan before you start each essay, to get in practice for the test.

1 *Act I Scene 2 lines 189–241*
Act III Scene 3 lines 41–102

What different impressions do we get of Ariel in these two extracts?

2 *Act I Scene 2 lines 425–end of the scene*
Act III Scene 1 lines 1–76

What impression do we get of the developing relationship between Ferdinand and Miranda in these two extracts?

3 *Act I Scene 2 lines 66–132*
Act II Scene 1 lines 139–64

What do you think Shakespeare is saying about the difficulties of governing in these two extracts?

4 *Act I Scene 2 lines 376–421*
Act III Scene 3 lines 18–102

Looking at the two extracts, write about whether you think magic is a force for good or bad in the play.

5 *Act I Scene 2 lines 311–72*
Act III Scene 2 lines 122–end of the scene

What different impressions of the island do we get from the language used in these two extracts?

6 *Act IV Scene 1 lines 139–64*
Act V Scene 1 lines 1–57

How does Shakespeare use language to suggest that Prospero has created a magic show or performance in the two extracts?

7 *Act I Scene 2 lines 244–99*
Act V Scene 1 lines 57–102

How would you advise the actor playing Prospero to perform in the following two extracts in order to bring out his different feelings?

8 *Act I Scene 1 (complete scene)*
Act I Scene 2 lines 1–54

If you were directing the play, how would you create a difference between these two extracts?

LITERARY TERMS

alliteration a sequence of words which all begin with the same letter (i.e. long lost love)

audience people watching a play

backdrop painted cloth hung at the back of the stage

character(s) either a person in a play, novel etc., or his or her personality

comedy a type of literature that is humorous and usually light hearted

connectives words or **phrases** that link ideas or sentences, such as 'However', 'in the same way', etc.

contradiction when something doesn't seem to make sense

contrast difference

costume items of clothing worn by the actors

debate discussion of an issue or problem

director the person responsible for the way a play is acted and **interpreted**

dramatic irony when the **audience** know more than the **characters** on the stage

Epilogue an extra speech by a **character** after the play has ended

exit leave (the stage)

extended metaphor a comparison which uses the same idea more than once

Fate future events which have been caused by chance or, in drama, sometimes by the action of gods

function the part something or someone plays in a drama

image (imagery) an image is a picture created in the mind by the use of language. The picture gives more meaning to an idea. Imagery is the use of these pictures in a piece of writing

impact the powerful effect that a word, **phrase** or event has on the **characters** and **audience**

imperative a verb that gives an order or command ('Go', 'Tell', etc.)

interlude a break, or interruption, in the main story

interpret to find your own meaning in a **text**

metaphor a direct comparison

mime acting without speech

monologue a single, long speech by one **character**

motivation a **character**'s reason for acting in a particular way

myths (mythical) legends or traditional stories (called myths), often Greek or Roman. The word mythical refers to these

off-stage out of sight of the **audience**

performance the play as it is acted, rather than as a written **text**

phrase a groups of words which don't make a full sentence

physical comedy **comedy** which uses movements and gestures for effect

plot the story-line of the play

plotters **characters** planning a trick or event in a play

poetry a type of writing that usually uses **rhythm** and **rhyme**, and is set out in lines rather than sentences

production the business of putting on a play, including the **performance**

prose   ordinary speech or writing, not **poetry**

quotation   exact words or **phrases** taken from the play and used in an essay to make a point

revelation   the moment when something important is revealed to the **audience**

rhyme   the use of words which have the same or similar sounds in one or more lines of **verse**

rhymed couplet   two lines of **verse** in which both lines **rhyme**

rhythm   the 'beat' or patterns of sound in speech

role   part in a play

scene   a part of an Act in a play

scenery   the **backdrop** and other furniture that make up the set on a stage

setting   where a play, or part of it, takes place

side-kick   a follower of a main **character**

simile   a suggested comparison using 'like' or 'as'

slapstick humour   **comedy** which is physical and often ridiculous (such as falling over)

soap opera   a type of drama on television which is focused on a specific place and the same group of people

sound effects   a sound which creates an effect on stage, e.g. thunder or explosions

special effects   visual effects usually used in film and television productions, such as making people disappear or changing their appearance over time

stage directions   the part of the script, provided by the writer, that suggests how the **characters** should move, speak, etc.

staging   putting on a play

sub plot   a story-line which is less important than the main one

symbol (symbolic)   something that is meant to represent an idea, e.g. a heart is a symbol of love

text   the play as it is written on paper

themes   the messages or ideas within a play

tone   the emotions, mood or atmosphere created on stage by the choice and sound of the language

tongue-twister   a **phrase** or **rhyme** which is very difficult to say quickly (i.e. 'She sells sea-shells on the sea-shore')

tragic   usually with an unhappy, or cruel ending

verbal   to do with speech

verse   lines written with a specific length and set to a **rhythm**, like **poetry**

CHECKPOINT HINTS/ANSWERS

CHECKPOINT 1
- Because of the lack of special effects available to theatres.

CHECKPOINT 2
- Sycorax, the witch who had imprisoned Ariel there, had died.

CHECKPOINT 3
- Ariel is described as 'moody' by Prospero (I.2.244) and seems to have feelings about wanting to be free.
- Ariel even seems moved by the tears of Gonzalo in Act V Scene 1, so he is not without feelings.

CHECKPOINT 4
- On the one hand, we are told Prospero treats Caliban like a 'slave' and punishes him, and that once Caliban 'loved' Prospero.
- On the other, we find out that Caliban tried to 'violate' Miranda, and that he has not turned his education to good use.

CHECKPOINT 5
- Gonzalo's 'commonwealth' is shown to be fairly unrealistic.
- Prospero perhaps tried to create an island of equals but Shakespeare seems to suggest that there will always be people – or creatures – who want to destroy things, or want more power than they are given (such as Antonio and Sebastian).

CHECKPOINT 6
- Gonzalo is innocent of any crime, and Prospero would prefer to deal with Alonso in his own way.
- Also, knowing that Antonio and Sebastian planned to kill them, is useful evidence for Prospero of their guilt.

CHECKPOINT 7
- Caliban was born on the island.
- Only Ariel has a similar knowledge of the island, and perhaps Prospero – with Ariel's help.

CHECKPOINT 8
- 'Wolves', 'bears', a 'raven', 'toads', 'beetles' and 'bats' are all mentioned in Act I Scene 2. Later, we hear about 'hedgehogs', 'adders' and, strangely, 'apes' (Act II Scene 2) although these are the forms spirits take to 'torment' Caliban.

CHECKPOINT 9
- 'Infected' suggests it is like a sickness – and cannot be controlled. At this stage, it might also suggest that Prospero disapproves.

CHECKPOINT 10
- It is not clear one way or the other. At one point, Prospero tells Ariel to become 'like a nymph of the sea' (I.2.301–2) but stops short of referring to Ariel as male or female. However, in myths nymphs are female.

CHECKPOINT 11
- 'Fury' and 'Tyrant' are aggressive words, the first meaning 'anger' and the second a powerful dictator or slave-driver. This perhaps fits with them chasing the three plotters away. 'Mountain' and 'Silver' sound like names someone might give dogs according to their size or appearance.

CHECKPOINT 12
- Probably not. Ariel has kept an eye on them, and they are so drunk and foolish it is unlikely their plan would succeed.

CHECKPOINT 13
- We – and Prospero – know that Ferdinand is alive. Also, we are aware that when Prospero talks about having 'lost' a daughter he is referring to her becoming Ferdinand's wife.

CHECKPOINT 14
- The game of chess is appropriate because the aim is to capture the king. This is what Prospero has done by capturing Alonso. You might also think the play is like a game of chess because Prospero is planning his moves like a chess player.

CHECKPOINT 15
- Prospero has no right to control Ariel. However, there is a tradition in stories that genies and spirits have to serve the person who has freed them. Prospero, of course, freed Ariel from the tree.

CHECKPOINT 16
- We should probably view Prospero as basically 'good' even if he can be cruel to Caliban. Think about how he was treated by Antonio and Alonso in Milan, and how he forgives them.

CHECKPOINT 17
- Prospero didn't choose to be on the island. Now that he has a dukedom to return to, there doesn't seem any point in staying.

CHECKPOINT 18
- Miranda has never seen any men other than her father – he is worried she hasn't seen who else is available! It is also possible he might be afraid of losing her.

CHECKPOINT 19
- Younger people do fall in love easily. In this case it may be physical attraction to start with, which grows into love.

CHECKPOINT 20
- Probably Prospero. Ferdinand is the son of a king, and therefore Prospero's grandchildren will one day be rulers of Naples, as well as (perhaps) Milan.

CHECKPOINT 21
- There is no specific evidence of its powers in the play. However, Prospero often appears 'unseen' or 'invisible' on several occasions – perhaps it can make him invisible when he needs it to?

CHECKPOINT 22
- Quite a lot. Prospero is only able to catch his enemies because they happen to be on a voyage by ship that comes close to his island. He even says it is 'strange, bountiful Fortune' (I.2.178) that has brought them to him.

CHECKPOINT 23
- On the one hand, the storm seems tropical and Ariel mentions the 'still-vexed Bermudas' (I.2.229), then talks about the 'Mediterranean' and later mentions 'coral'. However, there are also references in Act I Scene 2 to 'wolves', 'winters', and a 'fen' (a bog or marsh) on the island!

CHECKPOINT 24
- It must be quite small. Alonso and company search the whole island for Ferdinand, and Ariel is able to lead the same group on foot to Prospero.

CHECKPOINT 25
- Very different. Prospero and Miranda's conversation is not very exciting – just one

person telling a story – and would not have the same dramatic **impact** as the storm scene.

CHECKPOINT 26

- As they are under a spell, it might be that they are moving in a dream-like manner rather than making violent movements.

CHECKPOINT 27

- It may appear as if it has nothing to do with the main story and therefore will make an audience impatient to find out what will happen next.

CHECKPOINT 28

- There are many. Alonso and company learn that Prospero is alive, and so is Ferdinand. They also learn that Prospero has a daughter and that she is going to marry Ferdinand.
- They find out that Stephano and Trinculo were planning, with Caliban, to kill Prospero.

- It is also revealed that the ship and the crew are all unharmed and that Prospero intends to return to Milan to become duke.
- We find out that Ariel will be free once he performs his final tasks.

CHECKPOINT 29

- It is difficult to see Caliban as a simple villain or victim. He *is* complicated because it is very hard to understand a creature who tries, on the one hand, to attack Miranda and yet speaks so beautifully of the island and his dreams.

CHECKPOINT 30

- Simple actions such as a clenched fist or raising his hand as if to cast a spell would suggest Prospero's power in the first extract. In the second, laying his hand gently on Gonzalo's shoulder would make him seem kinder.

TEST ANSWERS

TEST YOURSELF

ACT I

1. Boatswain

2. Sebastian

3. Ariel

4. Caliban

5. Prospero

6. It has been twelve years since Prospero was Duke of Milan.

7. Ariel hides the ship in a harbour with the crew asleep under a spell.

8. He will be given his freedom.

9. Miranda taught Caliban to speak.

10. Prospero casts a spell on Ferdinand and forces him to drop his sword.

ACT II

1. Alonso

2. Gonzalo

3. Antonio

4. Caliban

5. Stephano

6. He saw Ferdinand swim powerfully in the waves and 'beat the surges under him'.

7. He would no longer have to pay a 'tribute' (a tax) to Alonso.

8. Trinculo seeks shelter because of the storm he thinks is coming, and the lack of any other shelter nearby.

9. Trinculo recognises Stephano's voice.

10. Stephano has given Caliban 'celestial liquor' (wine, in fact!) which he thinks comes from heaven. Caliban is also grateful that Stephano assumes he is some sort of being from another world, perhaps the moon, rather than a mere slave or monster.

ACT III

1. Miranda

2. Ferdinand

3. Trinculo

4. Caliban

5. Ariel

6. Caliban says the following can be used to kill Prospero: 'a nail' (knocked into his head), 'a log' (to 'batter his skull'), a 'stake', or a 'knife'.

7. Caliban, Trinculo and Stephano are lead off by a tune played by Ariel on a pipe, accompanied by a drum.

8. 'A table with rich food' is placed before Alonso and his companions.

9. Ariel becomes a harpy – a monstrous bird of prey.

10. Alonso believes he has heard the name of Prospero in the sound of thunder. This reminds him of the part he played in overthrowing him.

ACT IV

1. Ferdinand

TEST ANSWERS

2. Prospero

3. Trinculo

4. Caliban

5. Prospero

6. Prospero puts on the show as a form of wedding gift and also to show off his skills – some 'vanity of mine Art' as he calls it (IV.1.41).

7. Prospero suddenly remembers Caliban's plot to murder him and decides he needs to deal with it.

8. Ariel punishes them by dragging them through gorse bushes and thorns, and through 'filthy mantled pools' so that when they arrive they stink and are very uncomfortable.

9. Firstly, because Stephano seems more concerned about losing his bottles of drink, and then by their attraction to the glittering clothes hanging up.

10. The spirits take the form of hunting dogs.

ACT V

1. Prospero

2. Ariel

3. Alonso

4. Miranda

5. Caliban

6. Prospero has the power to reveal their plots against Alonso.

7. They are playing chess.

8. They are wearing the flashy clothes they stole from Prospero.

9. Prospero and Miranda will go back to Milan.

10. The audience can set Prospero free by applauding – with the 'help of your good hands'.

GCSE

Maya Angelou
I Know Why the Caged Bird Sings

Jane Austen
Pride and Prejudice

Alan Ayckbourn
Absent Friends

Elizabeth Barrett Browning
Selected Poems

Robert Bolt
A Man for All Seasons

Harold Brighouse
Hobson's Choice

Charlotte Brontë
Jane Eyre

Emily Brontë
Wuthering Heights

Brian Clark
Whose Life is it Anyway?

Robert Cormier
Heroes

Shelagh Delaney
A Taste of Honey

Charles Dickens
David Copperfield
Great Expectations
Hard Times
Oliver Twist
Selected Stories

Roddy Doyle
Paddy Clarke Ha Ha Ha

George Eliot
Silas Marner
The Mill on the Floss

Anne Frank
The Diary of a Young Girl

William Golding
Lord of the Flies

Oliver Goldsmith
She Stoops to Conquer

Willis Hall
The Long and the Short and the Tall

Thomas Hardy
Far from the Madding Crowd
The Mayor of Casterbridge
Tess of the d'Urbervilles
The Withered Arm and other Wessex Tales

L. P. Hartley
The Go-Between

Seamus Heaney
Selected Poems

Susan Hill
I'm the King of the Castle

Barry Hines
A Kestrel for a Knave

Louise Lawrence
Children of the Dust

Harper Lee
To Kill a Mockingbird

Laurie Lee
Cider with Rosie

Arthur Miller
The Crucible
A View from the Bridge

Robert O'Brien
Z for Zachariah

Frank O'Connor
My Oedipus Complex and Other Stories

George Orwell
Animal Farm

J. B. Priestley
An Inspector Calls
When We Are Married

Willy Russell
Educating Rita
Our Day Out

J. D. Salinger
The Catcher in the Rye

William Shakespeare
Henry IV Part I
Henry V
Julius Caesar
Macbeth
The Merchant of Venice
A Midsummer Night's Dream
Much Ado About Nothing
Romeo and Juliet
The Tempest
Twelfth Night

George Bernard Shaw
Pygmalion

Mary Shelley
Frankenstein

R. C. Sherriff
Journey's End

Rukshana Smith
Salt on the Snow

John Steinbeck
Of Mice and Men

Robert Louis Stevenson
Dr Jekyll and Mr Hyde

Jonathan Swift
Gulliver's Travels

Robert Swindells
Daz 4 Zoe

Mildred D. Taylor
Roll of Thunder, Hear My Cry

Mark Twain
Huckleberry Finn

James Watson
Talking in Whispers

Edith Wharton
Ethan Frome

William Wordsworth
Selected Poems
A Choice of Poets
Mystery Stories of the Nineteenth Century including The Signalman
Nineteenth Century Short Stories
Poetry of the First World War
Six Women Poets

For the AQA Anthology:
Duffy and Armitage & Pre-1914 Poetry
Heaney and Clarke & Pre-1914 Poetry
Poems from Different Cultures

Key Stage 3

William Shakespeare
Henry V
Macbeth
Much Ado About Nothing
Richard III
The Tempest

Margaret Atwood
Cat's Eye
The Handmaid's Tale
Jane Austen
Emma
Mansfield Park
Persuasion
Pride and Prejudice
Sense and Sensibility
William Blake
Songs of Innocence and of Experience
Charlotte Brontë
Jane Eyre
Villette
Emily Brontë
Wuthering Heights
Angela Carter
Nights at the Circus
Wise Children
Geoffrey Chaucer
The Franklin's Prologue and Tale
The Merchant's Prologue and Tale
The Miller's Prologue and Tale
The Prologue to the Canterbury Tales
The Wife of Bath's Prologue and Tale
Samuel Coleridge
Selected Poems
Joseph Conrad
Heart of Darkness
Daniel Defoe
Moll Flanders
Charles Dickens
Bleak House
Great Expectations
Hard Times
Emily Dickinson
Selected Poems
John Donne
Selected Poems
Carol Ann Duffy
Selected Poems
George Eliot
Middlemarch
The Mill on the Floss
T. S. Eliot
Selected Poems
The Waste Land
F. Scott Fitzgerald
The Great Gatsby

E. M. Forster
A Passage to India
Charles Frazier
Cold Mountain
Brian Friel
Making History
Translations
William Golding
The Spire
Thomas Hardy
Jude the Obscure
The Mayor of Casterbridge
The Return of the Native
Selected Poems
Tess of the d'Urbervilles
Nathaniel Hawthorne
The Scarlet Letter
Seamus Heaney
Selected Poems from 'Opened Ground'
Homer
The Iliad
The Odyssey
Aldous Huxley
Brave New World
Kazuo Ishiguro
The Remains of the Day
Ben Jonson
The Alchemist
James Joyce
Dubliners
John Keats
Selected Poems
Philip Larkin
The Whitsun Weddings and Selected Poems
Christopher Marlowe
Doctor Faustus
Edward II
Ian McEwan
Atonement
Arthur Miller
Death of a Salesman
John Milton
Paradise Lost Books I & II
Toni Morrison
Beloved
George Orwell
Nineteen Eighty-Four
Sylvia Plath
Selected Poems
Alexander Pope
Rape of the Lock & Selected Poems

William Shakespeare
Antony and Cleopatra
As You Like It
Hamlet
Henry IV Part I
King Lear
Macbeth
Measure for Measure
The Merchant of Venice
A Midsummer Night's Dream
Much Ado About Nothing
Othello
Richard II
Richard III
Romeo and Juliet
The Taming of the Shrew
The Tempest
Twelfth Night
The Winter's Tale
George Bernard Shaw
Saint Joan
Mary Shelley
Frankenstein
Bram Stoker
Dracula
Jonathan Swift
Gulliver's Travels and A Modest Proposal
Alfred Tennyson
Selected Poems
Alice Walker
The Color Purple
John Webster
The Duchess of Malfi
Oscar Wilde
The Importance of Being Earnest
Tennessee Williams
A Streetcar Named Desire
The Glass Menagerie
Jeanette Winterson
Oranges Are Not the Only Fruit
Virginia Woolf
To the Lighthouse
William Wordsworth
The Prelude and Selected Poems
W. B. Yeats
Selected Poems
Metaphysical Poets